A Mighty
CHANGE

Please Don't Let
My Baby Die

LORI WOOD

BookWise
publishing

A Mighty Change: Please Don't Let My Baby Die
Lori Wood

BookWise Publishing
3138 Matterhorn Drive
West Jordan, UT 84084
www.bookwisepublishing.com

Book design: Francine Eden Platt, Eden Graphics, Salt Lake City, Utah

Cover art: Mi Angel by Lori Wood

Library of Congress Cataloging: Pending

LCN 2010912739

ISBN: 978-1-60645-062-8

10 9 8 7 6 5 4 3 2 1

First Printing

PRINTED IN THE UNITED STATES OF AMERICA

Dedication

To my wonderful husband Lyle—not only did he live
this heartache with me; but without the countless hours
he spent by my side and his loving encouragement,
I could not have completed the work on this book.

Contents

Contents

Foreword

*H*ow can the death of your beloved child be one of the *greatest blessings of your life?* That is exactly what Lori wondered as she faced the challenge every parent prays they never have to face. This true story takes you through the horror and pain she experienced both before and after Brant's drowning and death. What would you do? How would you react? Would you be bitter at God and life? Would you blame your spouse for the tragedy? Would you fight the growth of new life experience? Is it even possible to make such an experience a positive growth experience? And more importantly, how do you do that?

As the ambulance paramedics carried her son's seemingly lifeless body into the hospital, her cry to them was, "Please, don't let my baby die." However, as she continued through the hospital stay, too often with loneliness as her only companion, Lori soon learned *it is not up to us,* a special message she received from her dying son.

Through Lori's continued journey in life with her husband by her side, they found they could cope with this unforeseen tragedy. They discovered as they turned to their seven children for comfort that they are taught by them individually and collectively, providing answers to questions such as how do we separate the cliché "it is not up to us" from "after all we can do"? What things are out of our control, and what things must we do to work out our life's mission, and then "be still"? Their personal answers are shared within the pages of this book.

Lori has found so much goodness in others who served her and her family. As experience after experience unfolds, so do the tentacles of pain that are wrapped around Lori's heart. She finds peace and solace as she ponders the teachings of so many others that have gone through this reluctant and frightening sojourn. Words of comfort are spoken to her by friends or acquaintances and even onlookers. The written word through books and articles, guides her inner soul to receive divine council. Her conclusion is *yes, there are angels among us, some we may not be able to see, and others that cross our path daily* . . . and this was *the greatest blessing of her life* as it continues to mold her into the person she is becoming.

Acknowledgements

There are so many angels that come to your rescue in a time of need. I wish I could have acknowledged all of them in my story, but that would not have been possible. I would like to name a few now and share the story behind each angel.

Allyson Wood, my sister-in-law who without thinking twice, dropped all she was doing after Brant's funeral and came to stay with us for a week. Allyson had three small children of her own at the time, yet she left the older children with her husband, a five hour drive away and brought her very small baby with her to take care of us. The pain I felt that first week was so deep, I almost couldn't move. She made every meal we ate and completely cared for our children. Thank you, Allyson. You will always hold a dear place in my heart.

Brother and Sister Fred Lang were people who never stopped serving. As I mention in my book, they were some of the first who came to our home to offer words of comfort. Later I learned they were the ones behind the sack lunches that not only fed us after Brant's funeral, but for many weeks beyond.

Henrietta Archibald was a woman of constant service. Her husband was later our bishop, and she had a son Kyle's age. She gave me a small hand-stitched, framed tapestry with Brant's name embroidered on it; I have it to this day. When my doctor ordered me to complete bed rest in the last trimester of my pregnancy with Tomi, Henrietta came over regularly to clean my home and take care of Kyle and Angela. She convinced Kyle to help her clean by suggesting he could have any money he found while cleaning. She may have been a greater inspiration to Kyle for years to come than she could ever know. Kyle started finding ways to earn money (on a grand scale) by the age of seven and has never quit.

Sister Swartz was a majestic, beautiful woman who wasn't afraid to get her hands dirty. She was one who volunteered to clean my house during my pregnancy with Tomi. She came in my room one day in her gorgeous, yellow, 'Liz Claiborne' outfit and asked—no demanded—I give her a job to do. Shocked at her lovely, yet strong appearance, I said something like, "I have no idea what my house needs; I haven't been out of bed in weeks." She responded with, "Okay, I'll clean your bathroom." At that she proceeded to pull on her yellow latex gloves, picked up her bucket of cleaning supplies, and headed into my bathroom. Within half an hour she came back out. I could smell the aroma of the cleaning products follow her out as she announced, "Your bathroom is clean. Is there anything else you need done?" I assured her she had done all she needed to. She wished me well and left. It left me with a valuable lesson on charity I have never forgotten—it doesn't matter your state in life, you are never above, or overdressed for service.

—Lori Wood

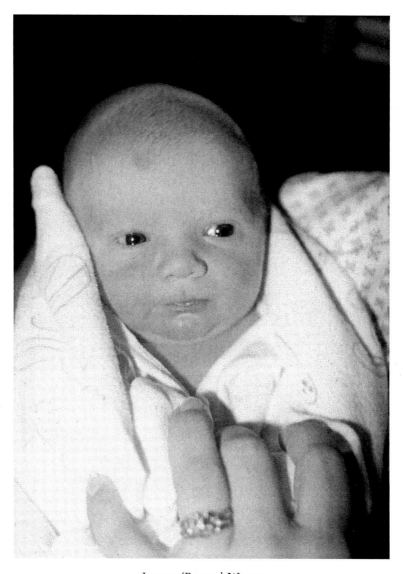

LESTER 'BRANT' WOOD

Please Don't Let My Baby Die

*M*ortal life is a wonderful experience. However, in retrospect, one might view this experience as something they would never recover or heal from. As I look back over the past twenty-three years, there is a silver lining on a very dark cloud. It truly has become one of the greatest blessings of my life. How can the death of your beloved child be a blessing? As hard as it is to still think about, let me go back and share with you the experience that changed my life and the lives of my family.

> *The greatest work you will ever do will be within the walls of your own home.*
> — HAROLD B. LEE —

On October 10, 1985, my morning started in what seemed to be complete chaos. I preferred that my children do their chores before school, but that morning seemed especially difficult. I was three months pregnant with our sixth child and very, very sick. With little to no cooperation from my three older kids, in frustration, I lost my temper, which consisted of an elevated voice, a few threats of privileges being suspended, and "I guess you'll just have to do your chores after school." I then let my children leave for school with my anger hanging over their heads, something I really hated to do.

Surprisingly, that day I felt better than usual by mid-morning, so I decided to clean the kitchen floor. I don't think it had been cleaned since I started getting sick. The floor was large and I liked to clean it on my hands and knees. I put a gate up to the entrance of the kitchen so my three and a half year old son Kyle, who always was a little more help than I needed while I was cleaning, and my sixteen-month-old son Brant, a very vivacious, adorable toe head, wouldn't walk all over the wet floor. They stood at the gate and watched and I got joy out of knowing that if they could, they would be kneeling by my side. I felt a good spirit settle in my home as I worked.

My father, who was the owner and operator of a long haul truck, had just brought us a box of fresh Oregon apples a couple of days before, and the boys loved them. I suggested they eat an apple while they watched. As I neared the end of the job, I told Kyle to start putting on his and Brant's shoes. I needed to run some errands, and I wanted to pick up my other children for lunch as a surprise. I planned to keep them with me the remainder of the day, to repair feelings, from the sour morning we had. Kyle did as I asked and Brant followed him, as Brant always did. The boys were best friends. Kyle was Brant's 'self appointed' protector and guide in life. Brant was too young to put on his own shoes, but I knew it would keep Kyle busy for a few minutes, as Kyle tried to help him. They disappeared into the family room and I finished the kitchen floor.

> *You can gain strength, courage and confidence by every experience in which you really stop to look fear in the face . . . .You must do the thing which you think you cannot do.*
>
> — ELEANOR ROOSEVELT —

As I completed my task just a couple of minutes later, I called for them. Kyle came but Brant didn't. I asked Kyle to go get Brant. I needed to input into the computer a couple of insurance cost comparisons (a home business I had) which would take about two minutes. As I finished, Kyle came in and said he couldn't find Brant. For some reason, fear immediately struck my heart, even though it had only been about ten minutes since Brant was standing at the kitchen door. He had figured out how to open the front door because it had a lever handle, and I pictured him in our not yet landscaped front yard, with stickers in his feet.

The strange thing was, even though that was the picture that came to my mind, I passed the front door and went through the family room, towards the Jacuzzi room. My heart was pounding, and I could hardly breathe. The door to the bathroom that led to the Jacuzzi room was open. Brant couldn't open this door yet because of the round antique door knobs it had, and we always kept the door shut; Brant would play in the toilet if we didn't. I entered the bathroom and I saw the door to the Jacuzzi room was also open. This door was also always kept closed and dead-bolted, for obvious reasons, but that morning a repairman had been working on the Jacuzzi. My heart was in my throat as I rushed in. To add to my shock, the cover on it was pulled halfway back. When I first glanced at the Jacuzzi, I didn't see anything. Then I noticed there was something floating under the cover. At first it looked like a piece of clothing and yet I felt a need to pull the cover back further. To my horror, it was my son! I grabbed him by one arm to pull him out, at the same time screaming, "No! No! Please no!" I had a strange feeling come over me; I just wanted to run. I didn't know where I would run or why I would feel that way.

> *Whether you think that you can, or that you can't, you are usually right.*
> — HENRY FORD —

I quickly realized I had to get control of myself and do something fast.

Brant's skin was pasty-looking and felt tight and swollen. I laid him on the floor, trying to remember what I learned in ninth grade health class on rescue breathing. I remembered I needed to tilt his head back. I didn't even think to check for a pulse. I just started pushing in the area of his chest I felt was the right place. As I did, water gushed from his mouth. As soon as it was clear of the water, I breathed into his mouth. I saw his chest lift slightly. I thought I was supposed to push the air back out, so I pushed on his chest, which ended up being an ideal response since I didn't even think about giving him CPR.

After a few breaths I felt I needed to take him into the family room. I picked him up, carried him in and laid him on the floor. I was shocked at how heavy he was. I was accustomed to carrying him all the time, but now he felt so much heavier. I once again began the rescue breathing. By this time, my three-and a-half year old came in. He stood and watched as I cried out Brant's name and again pressed on his chest. In his fears and innocence, he began shaking Brant's leg and saying his name over and over. This upset me; I snapped at him and asked him to "please stop!"

I knew at this point I needed help. I didn't feel I could stop breathing for Brant long enough to call someone for help. My phone rang during this period of time, but I didn't dare leave him to an-

> *Where can I turn for peace?*
> *Where is my solace?*
> *When other sources cease,*
> *To make me whole?*
> *When with a wounded heart,*
> *Anger, or malice,*
> *I draw myself apart,*
> *Searching my soul?*
>
> *Where, when my aching grows,*
> *Where, when I languish,*
> *Where, in my need to know,*
> *Where can I run?*
> *Where is the quiet hand*
> *To calm my anguish?*
> *Who, who can understand?*
> *He, only one.*
>
> *He answers privately,*
> *Reaches my reaching*
> *In my Gethsemane,*
> *Savior and Friend.*
> *Gentle the peace he finds*
> *For my beseeching.*
> *Constant he is and kind,*
> *Love without end.*
>
> — EMMA LOU THAYNE

swer it and ask for help. Now I felt I didn't have a choice. I would need to send my little son, Kyle, for help. I understand now that I've been trained in rescue breathing and CPR, I should have called for help immediately, but in my mind at the time, I didn't think that was an option.

We lived in the outskirts of Las Vegas on half acre lots, so for a little one, the neighbors weren't close by. I only knew one neighbor well enough to send my young son for help. They lived through a wash and around the corner, facing the other street. I needed to watch Kyle to make sure he understood and would be safe, so I again picked up Brant, this time carrying him out in the garage. I laid him on a large carpet roll, which was in the garage, waiting for carpet layers to put in our basement. From there, I could watch Kyle until he went around the corner to the front of their house.

As I continued to breathe for Brant, I noticed little red dots starting to form all over his face. They looked like tiny blood blisters, pin point in size. They were bright red in color, not dark red like a blood blister would be. I somehow knew Brant was not getting enough oxygen. I have since learned this happens when bleeding under the skin occurs due to the lack of oxygen in the body's system, as in asphyxiation or suffocation. I worked harder. Kyle came back and said there wasn't anyone home. I felt so alone! What could I do? We had new neighbors on the south side of us, but I hadn't met them yet. They were young and looked nice so I instructed Kyle to go there and ask for help. I again watched, but knew I couldn't wait. I feared my son was dying.

I picked Brant up again, this time going to the kitchen, where the phone was. I laid him on the bench beside the table. I breathed for him again and then grabbed the phone. I dialed the operator since 911 was not in existence then. When I heard the operator's voice, I could feel the extra power I'd had with me up to this point leaving me. I wasn't sure I could talk. I mustered all I had and almost yelled into the phone, "My baby drowned. I think he's dying."

I heard her tense response, "I'll connect you to the fire department."

As the fire department answered, I repeated, "My baby drowned. I think he's dying." My voice was so strained, it sounded strange to me. She asked my location. I gave her my address, and then somehow I knew I needed to immediately follow with the major cross streets. I hung up the phone and again began rescue breathing.

> *Love and gratitude can part seas, they can move mountains, and they can create miracles.*
>
> — UNKNOWN —

Just then Kyle came in with our neighbor. She was a very pretty young woman, maybe twenty-four. I was so relieved to see her. I hoped she would know what to do. Through my tears, I managed to ask her what I should do. She looked at me with sadness and panic and said, "I don't know any more than what you're doing!" I so hoped she could take over, but I knew I just needed to keep going myself. As I continued with the rescue breathing, I heard the distant sound of a siren.

My neighbor said, "I'll go wave them down." I was very grateful for that.

I remember thinking how surprised I was that the ambulance arrived so quickly. I've always heard in these situations that it seems to take the ambulance forever to get there. I learned later that the fire department was only a mile or so away, and they were dispatched immediately. I believe it was five minutes or less for their arrival. I cannot describe the relief I felt as they came into my kitchen and took over. They asked permission to take Brant out to their truck where they had the equipment they needed, as well as a better place to work on him. "Of course," I said, and they whisked him away. I suddenly felt so helpless and empty. At last I could really cry, but I'm not sure I did; I was too numb. My neighbor put her arm around me as we followed them out.

My son, Kyle, had his arms around my leg.

The paramedic met us at the garage and asked permission to cut Brant's shirt off him. He said it was in the way of whatever equipment they needed to use on him. I felt it was a strange request—*why would they even ask?* I said they could do whatever they needed to do. He then said they needed to transport him to the hospital, just as another ambulance arrived.

I could see through the small side window of the fire department ambulance that the paramedics were frantically working on my son. I asked one of the paramedics if I could go with them. He said yes but I would need to sit in the front so I wouldn't be in the way. I didn't want to be in the back for that very reason. I was very glad to let someone else completely take over what I had been attempting to do. My neighbor immediately said she would keep Kyle and for me not to worry about him. I again felt so grateful for this sweet angel I had never met until right then. I knew Kyle would be safe with her. Kyle was very attached to me, but for some reason was so grown up at that moment, and just willingly took her hand as I climbed into the truck.

As the driver climbed in and started to back the truck up, he revealed his own panic as he backed into the other ambulance. He quickly went forward and just drove through the front yard area which wasn't landscaped yet.

> ## ANGELS
>
> *Angels are the guardians of hope and wonder, the keepers of magic and dreams.*
> *Angels watch over you wherever you go, keeping each day perfect and promising a bright new tomorrow.*
> *The motto of all angels is "It's a wonderful life."*
> *Wherever there is love; an angel is flying by. Angels help you carry the ball, carry a tune, carry your weight and carry on! Your guardian angel knows you inside and out and loves you just the way you are.*
> — UNKNOWN —

With sirens screaming, he headed for the nearest hospital which was about five or six miles away. The main street which led to the hospital was only a couple of blocks from our home. I was amazed at the lack of respect the drivers on this main road had for an ambulance. At one point, we were behind two cars side by side that were going the same direction as us. There were only two lanes, and the ambulance driver couldn't get around them. We followed the cars with the sirens blaring, and yet neither car even attempted to pull over. The driver began honking his "very loud" horn. Two women were in one car talking away. I couldn't believe they didn't seem to see or hear us. Finally, he was forced over to the center lane, as they both seemed oblivious to our presence. It was a real struggle to get to the hospital with the traffic so slow to respond and move out of the way. It was a complete shock for me to watch.

I looked through the window into the back of the truck, in hopes to see a more relaxed attitude, but it didn't happen; relaxed it was not. I couldn't see what was being done, nor could I see Brant, but I could see the EMTs in the back; they were bent over Brant and there was an anxious, intense attitude about them.

As we arrived at the hospital, the driver pulled straight in towards the emergency room doors rather than backing in. He said they wouldn't waste any time on a gurney; one of them would just carry him in. I stepped out of the truck and realized I didn't have any shoes or socks on.

Just then they brought my son around from the back of the truck, hurrying towards the emergency entrance doors. He was very pale and lifeless. I think this was the first time I really understood the reality of it all. It was cold outside, and I was wet from pulling Brant out of the water, yet I didn't feel cold—just empty.

A small group of people had gathered and were watching with curiosity, seeming as shocked at the sight of Brant's appearance as I was.

At that moment, I finally broke down. The emotion was beyond anything I had ever known before, my heart hurt to the depths of my soul; my body was wooden and I moved mechanically. I felt controlled by a greater power than my own; through my cries, my voice was weak and notably strained as I pleaded with the paramedics carrying him. "Please," I said, "please, don't let my baby die!"

I felt the driver's concern for me as we entered the hospital. A nurse rushed up and said something to the driver as the other paramedics with my son were ushered another direction. I heard the driver say to the nurse, "Get the mom. She's in bad shape."

I remember thinking I don't know why he would say that. I'm doing well, and I'm being strong. Then her arm went around me, for support, and I realized I was ready to collapse. She asked, "Are you okay?"

I looked at her, through tears, and said, "My baby needs a blessing." I felt that was the most important thing at that moment.

She asked, "What church?" Almost before my response was out of my mouth, she said, "I'll call the Elders." How did she know? I thought, but I didn't want to ask. I just continued to walk.

Is any sick among you? Let him call for the Elders of the church; and let them pray over him, anointing him with oil in the name of the Lord.
— JAMES 5:14 —

Coincidence or Divine Intervention?

The nurse led me to a very small room with a little couch, table, phone and chair. I was so cold at this point that I was shivering. She noticed that my feet were bare, and I was wet from holding my son. She said, "I'll bring you a blanket; just sit down here. Is there anyone I can call?"

I couldn't think; I felt so confused and blank. I could only respond with, "I don't know." She hurried out and came back a few moments later, with a warm blanket and a pair of little blue socks for my feet. She asked me again if there was someone she could call for me. I told her my husband was at an appointment (there were no cell phones then), and I could only remember my sister's phone number. She tried to call my sister for me but didn't get an answer. She showed me how to dial out on the phone so I could continue trying to call my sister, or anyone else, if I happened to remember any numbers. She left. Once again, I was all alone.

The room was silent and cold; I felt completely insecure in this place; I dialed my sister again . . . still no answer. I dialed my home, hoping

> *To some is given the gift of music, art, athleticism, knowledge . . . but to all—the ability to love, show compassion, be charitable, loving, patient, and kind.*
> — UNKNOWN —

my husband may have come home . . . no answer. I had several close friends I could call and knew their phone numbers very well, but as hard as I tried, I could not remember any one of them.

A different person came in—a male nurse. I felt like it had been a very long time, but it probably hadn't. He was so excited to inform me they had my son's heart beating on its own. *What?* I hadn't realized it wasn't beating. I hadn't even thought to check for a heartbeat. I was shocked and devastated—to think all this time his heart had not been beating. I'm sure the man who'd come to inform me wondered why I wasn't excited. *How could I be excited?* This meant it was so much worse than I had realized. Why hadn't I thought to check for a heartbeat? He then informed me they were still working on trying to get him to breathe on his own. He stood up and left the room. Once again I was left alone; feeling lonelier than ever.

> We learn and grow by overcoming challenges with faith, persistence, and personal righteousness.
> — ANN M. DIBB —

I picked up the phone again and called my home. *Lyle, please be home!* Still no answer. I knew he wouldn't be there; I wasn't expecting him home for hours. I racked my brain trying to remember anyone's phone number. *Why couldn't I think?*

The first nurse came in again. "The Elders are here," she informed me. "They can give your son a blessing right now. Please, come with me." She gently took my arm to lead me. I was so grateful; now everything would be okay. I would see my son and maybe someone who could give me answers.

I followed the nurse into a small room, near the doors we came in. The room was crowded with people working on my son. It felt so intimidating. There were doctors, paramedics and two men in suits.

They looked so familiar, but I didn't know why. The whole scene overwhelmed me as I watched them working on Brant. I hadn't expected such a sight. I'm not sure what I expected, but definitely not this. I didn't even dare speak.

The two Elders from my church were standing in the corner, near the door, as we walked in. The doctors stepped slightly aside, but seemed somewhat annoyed as they motioned the Elders over. One doctor told them to go ahead, but the doctors would need to continue so the Elders would need to try to stay as much out of the way as they could, as it was such a small room. I had to stay near the door, which was a few feet from the foot of the bed. They laid their hands on Brant's head, as much as they could without interrupting the doctors' work, and proceeded to anoint and bless him. I wasn't able to hear the blessing, as they spoke in a whisper. This was in respect for the sacredness of the blessing, as well as respect for the doctors' needing to focus on what they were doing. I wanted to hear what they said, and I strained to catch a word or two. I wondered if they had felt confident that Brant would recover. The blessing they gave was short, yet I was sure they said all that was needed to be said.

> *Sorrow looks back, worry looks around, and faith looks up.*
> — UNKNOWN —

As they came and stood by me, I remembered why the one looked so familiar to me. He was my Stake President. We had recently moved into the stake and so I had not seen him much or formally met him. I couldn't recall his name at the moment, but that wasn't surprising. I said, "Thank you so much, President." As I stumbled for words, I continued with, "I'm sorry I don't recall your name." I felt embarrassed.

He replied, "President Simmons." Then realizing I was in his stake, he asked, "Who's your bishop?"

I was, of course, blank. Apparently, the man with him knew me because he said, "Bishop Creel." I didn't recognize him but later my husband told me he was a member of our ward at church. President Simmons said he would call Bishop Creel, and then he asked me what else he could do. I told him I was worried about my other children. The older ones would be getting out of school soon, and would be expecting me to pick them up. I didn't like them riding the bus so I drove them to and from school every day. There were too many issues happening on the bus, and we decided a little inconvenience was worth protecting our children.

President Simmons said he would be happy to pick our kids up, but I knew they would not get in the car with him. We had drilled into our children not to get in a car with someone they didn't know, and they didn't know him. I again apologized because I did need his help.

He said, "No. That's good." He said he would call the school and inform them of the situation. He would have them keep the kids in the office until my sister could be contacted and pick them up. He took her name and phone number and assured me he would find her. I knew she would be home soon, as her own children would be coming home from school.

> *And he that searcheth the hearts knoweth what is the mind of the Spirit, because he maketh intercession for the Saints according to the will of God.*
> — ROMANS 8:27 —

At this time, the nurse respectfully asked President Simmons, his companion, and me if we could step out of the room. I'm not sure why, except possibly they were concerned about my hearing the discussion the doctors were having concerning the outcome of Brant's condition. We promptly left the room. President Simmons and his companion stayed with me as we waited.

A couple of interesting circumstances which I learned about later; is it a coincidence or divine intervention? You decide. The first interesting "coincidence" was the experience of President Simmons. I learned later that he and his companion were on the list at the hospital to be called if someone requested a blessing. Their office was located fairly close to the hospital, which made it possible for them to get there in a timely manner. President Simmons was a partner in a law firm, and his companion was one of the junior partners. It just so happened, on that day, his name had rotated to the top of the list. He said he would bring his own companion, who happened to be in his stake and happened to know us. They did not know when they left for the hospital who they would be giving a blessing to or why.

When President Simmons learned who I was, he realized he knew my uncle very well. When we parted, he not only called the school and my Bishop, but he also called my Uncle Lynn. He informed him that I was alone, and that my son's condition was very serious.

I was stunned when, by that evening, my mother's family was there or on their way. We are a close family, and we surround one another in times like these. My father, who had just come through town, was reached and was able to turn around and head back. My uncle contacted my mother, and she was on a flight from Oregon by that afternoon. It was when this amazing story was shared, that I realized how much we are cared for by our Father

> There is a first faith.
> And a second faith.
> The first faith is the easy,
> traditional belief
> of childhood,
> taken from other people,
> believed because it
> belonged to the
> time and land.
> The second faith is the
> personal conviction
> of the soul . . .
> It is the heart knowing,
> because God has spoken
> to it, the things of God . . .
> It and it alone, is the belief
> which brings salvation.
>
> — PHILLIPS BROOKS

in Heaven. He never leaves us alone. Unfortunately, we may leave him, but He never leaves us. Why was a man that happened to be my stake president, called first, and in turn, he recognized that I was related to his good friend in a town of hundreds of thousands of people. What are the odds?

The second "coincidence" regarded my sister. She had gone shopping that morning, and as she was shopping felt impressed to call me. She knew I was sick with my pregnancy but wanted to know if I felt well enough to meet her. As I said earlier, my phone rang while I was resuscitating Brant in the family room. I wanted to run and answer it but didn't dare leave Brant. It was my sister calling. She became concerned after a while and called again. My neighbor told us later she heard the phone ringing as the ambulance left. It was Gwen calling the second time. She lived on the other side of town, but had decided that morning to go to Mervyn's near us. She decided, since she was so close, she would drive the extra ten minutes to my home and check on me. This was an unusual thing for her to do, especially considering I hadn't answered my phone. It would have been logical to assume I was with Lyle. When she arrived, our neighbor saw her pull in and ran out with Kyle to meet her. The neighbor explained all that had happened and where I was. Gwen took Kyle and then felt she should go to the school for my other children.

For He shall
give His angels charge
over thee, to keep thee
in all thy ways.
— PSALMS 91:11 —

Angel in Green

The nurse came up again and explained they were going to need to transport Brant to another hospital. The doctors felt Brant's heart was stable at that time, but they couldn't improve his condition any further at this hospital. They knew they needed to move him to a facility that had the capability to handle his extremely critical condition. The other hospital had doctors and nurses who were experts in this type of trauma. She said they would transport him in a different ambulance. The ambulance that had arrived after the fire department's ambulance would take him this time. She also explained that because of his serious condition and the limited space, I would not be able to ride with him. However, she had arranged for transportation for me. She walked away momentarily, and my Stake President said he was going to leave but wanted me to know he would be trying to locate my husband and Bishop Creel. He didn't say anything about my uncle, which is why the story took me by surprise. They turned and left.

> *And whoso receiveth you, there I will be also, for I will go before your face. I will be on your right hand and on your left, and my Spirit shall be in your hearts, and mine angels round about you, to bear you up.*
> — Doctrine & Covenants 84:88 —

The nurse came back with a very kind looking woman at her side. The nurse introduced her, but I no longer remember her name. She was about my height (five feet two inches) maybe a little shorter, with short, reddish brown hair in an old-fashioned style with curls. I remember clearly she was wearing a green shirt. She looked as if she was about my mother's age, fifty-ish. I was told she was a volunteer at the hospital and was available for whatever service that was needed for families. In my case, that service was a ride to the other hospital, which was about thirty minutes away.

> *There is no obstacle to great, no challenge too difficult, if we have faith.*
> — GORDON B. HINCKLEY —

Just at that moment, they brought Brant out of the room on a gurney. I hardly had a chance to see him; they took him so quickly to the emergency doors. I watched as they went through the doors and lifted him up in the ambulance. His color was better, and he just seemed to be in a very deep sleep. There were tubes everywhere, including down his throat. I had to watch as they just took my baby away. The whole scene tore my heart out, and I started to cry. The woman was understanding and said, "Don't worry; I'll take you to him."

Just then the paramedics from the fire department came up to me. They were very sober, and the driver wished me good luck. I could see he was very troubled and couldn't manage to say any more than that. He seemed to sincerely hurt for me. I don't know if I felt good or bad about his gesture, as it didn't offer me much hope because of the distressed attitude he portrayed. I almost wished he hadn't said anything at all at the time, but later I appreciated the love and concern he showed.

The woman in green took my arm and guided me out. We went to her car. It was an older model car, which surprised me. I thought how awesome it was, as she didn't seem "well-to-do" financially, and yet here she was giving of her time and money by transporting me across town. She made small talk all the way to the other hospital. I have no idea what she said. I'm sure I heard her at the time, but all I could think of was the picture of my son over and over as they wheeled him from the hospital. I just wanted to put my arms around him and make it all better. I must admit I felt a little annoyed at her chatter, but I didn't want to be rude or ungrateful for her act of kindness. I pretended to listen, but I was really thinking of my son and the pain I was trying not to feel.

I thought of my other children. *Were they okay?* My oldest daughter, Darci, was only eleven. Courtney, our oldest son, was nine, and Matthew was seven. I hoped President Simmons had reached my sister and she had them. I felt so helpless. I wasn't even driving myself to the next hospital, and the woman that was driving me seemed to be driving so slowly. Bless her heart, but would we ever get to the hospital? I wanted so much at that moment for her to just stop talking and drive. I hope that doesn't seem heartless or ungrateful. The whole thing was so confusing; I didn't feel I was really living it. I seemed so detached from the situation, like I wasn't me; I was in someone else's life. The sun was shining, and it didn't seem right that it was. People were going here and there, and they didn't know my son's life was hanging in the balance.

We may never know in this life why we face what we do, but we can feel confident that we can grow from the experience.
— JAMES B. MARTINO —

At last, we arrived at the hospital. She seemed to know exactly where to park and where to go, like she had done this before. I realize now she probably had. I didn't have to think; I just followed her. Once again, I was very grateful for her and felt so bad I had thought negatively in any way about her. She headed through the lobby towards the elevators. She pushed the button to take us to the third floor. We left the elevator and turned right, going down the corridor nearly to the end. We came to a nurse's station. It was the nurse's station for the Pediatric Intensive Care Unit (PICU).

A doctor was there to meet us and asked if I was the mother. The volunteer said yes. He proceeded to talk to me as he introduced him-self— Dr. McCarthy. He was tall and fit, with dark hair. He had a kind and caring, but very intense look on his face. He began to tell me of Brant's condition. As he did, he motioned to an open door which was directly across from the nurse's station where we stood. Next to the door was a large glass window that looked into the room. The door was oversized, and I could see into the entire room. My son was lying on the hospital bed inside.

> *Things are how they are,*
> *and complaining doesn't help.*
> — JOHN H. GROBERG —

Dr. McCarthy began to explain they were setting up all the neces-sary life support equipment at that time so I couldn't see Brant yet. I found myself watching Brant. Dr. McCarthy would say "Mrs. Wood" to recapture my attention, and I would try to focus on what he was telling me, but again my head would drift back to the direction of Brant's room. I wasn't hearing most of what Dr. McCarthy was saying. My thoughts were in the room with my son. Finally, Dr. McCarthy said, "Mrs. Wood, I really need you to listen to what I'm saying. It's really important you understand." His voice was stern but compassionate. I turned my atten-tion to him, not daring to look at Brant until he gave me his permission. I felt like a child needing to obey instead of the mother of five children. He again tried to explain the medical procedures they were doing. They were going to drill a hole into Brant's head so they could insert a bolt that would monitor the pressure and swelling of Brant's brain. *What?*

But I didn't dare interrupt to ask why. I thought, *I'll ask later. I can't worry about technical terms or reasons right now.* I just wanted it all to end.

Dr. McCarthy then suggested that the volunteer take me down to the admittance offices and get the paperwork done. I couldn't believe this. *Are you kidding me? My son is lying in there near death, and you want me to go fill out paperwork?* I wanted to stay there, near my baby boy. What if he died while I was gone? Dr. McCarthy read the look of horror and shock on my face and explained that I couldn't go in at this time anyway. He said I would be in the way, and that taking care of the paperwork would be the best thing for me to do right now. Then he waved for the volunteer to take me away.

Again, I just followed. I didn't voice any of my thoughts. I couldn't get the words out anyway. I did feel everyone's compassion for me, and I was very touched by it. I knew they were directing me in the best way they could at the moment, so I went.

We went back down the same elevator to the lobby. As we stepped out, I looked forward, and walking towards the elevators was Bishop Creel. I was overwhelmed with a feeling of love and support. I called his name and ran towards him. At last, in seeing a face I knew, all of my emotions that were bottled inside came rushing to the surface. I began to sob hysterically. Bishop Creel put his arms around me. I could feel I was about to collapse. My knees felt so weak, but he held me up. I wondered how he could have arrived at the hospital so soon. How grateful I was for the quick links in our church.

The volunteer walked up and explained the situation to him, who she was, and where she was taking me. She asked him if he would like her to stay. He said no, that he would take care of things from this point. He thanked her for her kindness and help. She put her arm around me and told me she would pray for my son and then wished me well. She was so kind and tender. I thanked her, as much as I could manage to get out through my sobs, and she left.

I never saw her again. I was with her for only an hour, maybe an hour and a half, but I will never forget her face or her acts of kindness and charity. She, in that short time, became an important part of my life story. I am filled with emotion to tears, as I think of her, even now. It causes me to reflect on the things we do each day, the wasted time in selfish acts. If we truly do as the Savior taught and serve one another selflessly, we can all become angels, holding each other up in time of need, as this wonderful woman did for me. I hope she has received all that she truly deserves for her charity.

*Strangers are
just friends waiting
to happen.*
— MENCIUS —

He Prayed Aloud

Bishop Creel put his arm around me and directed me toward the admittance offices. As we walked, we passed a chapel. He asked if I would like to go in and say a prayer. I nodded my head yes.

We stepped into a small, dimly lit chapel. It had pews going up each side with a center aisle. As we walked to the front, I felt a little uncomfortable. It was different from the chapels I had been accustomed to. There was a picture of Christ on the wall in the front. I think the reason it felt different, now that I think about it, was because it was so dim. I was used to bright, well-lit chapels. I'm sure this served a purpose for this particular chapel, maybe allowing people that quiet time to feel they were alone with the Savior, as well as alone with their sorrow.

If only one prayer you said in your life was "thank-you" that would suffice.
— Meister Eckhart —

My bishop guided me to the front. We were alone, and I was grateful for that. We sat on a bench near the front. Bishop Creel asked if I would like him to offer a prayer. I definitely did want and needed him to pray. He said a sweet, simple prayer. He humbly petitioned the Lord for my comfort and then he prayed for my little son. My heart hurt. All I could think about was my baby. "Please, Heavenly Father, please, please," I

Dearest children, God is near you,
Watching o'er you day and night,
And delights to own and bless you,
If you strive to do what's right.
He will bless you; he will bless you,
If you put your trust in him.

Dearest children, holy angels
Watch your actions night and day,
And they keep a faithful record
Of the good and bad you say.
Cherish virtue, cherish virtue!
God will bless the pure in heart.

Children, God delights to teach you,
By his Holy Spirits voice.
Quickly heed its holy promptings,
Day by day you'll then rejoice.
Oh, prove faithful; oh prove faithful,
To your God and Zion's cause.

— CHARLES L. WALKER

pleaded in my mind as he prayed aloud, "don't take my son from me." I couldn't even bear the thought. Bishop Creel ended the prayer. We sat for a moment, but I felt anxious to go. I needed to get back to Brant. I know Bishop Creel could feel this because right on cue he suggested we leave.

We still needed to go to the registration office, which was near the chapel. We were immediately taken to an available person. She asked us to sit down. There were several stations with partitions between them for privacy. They went from the door we came in to the windows in the front. We were at the front and could see out the windows into the parking lot and front entrance of the hospital. The woman behind the desk began asking me questions: my name, my husband's name, my son's name, our address, and so on. She wanted our insurance information. I gave her the name of the company. What was our group number? She needed the card to make a copy of it, but I didn't have it. She seemed perturbed, "Why not?"

Unbelievable! I thought. I didn't think to put on shoes, let alone get my purse so I could have my insurance card handy. I didn't say anything to her. I just stared, not knowing what she wanted me to do. Giving my name and address was hard enough.

My bishop jumped in. "Can we get this to you later?"

She hesitated.

Just then I glanced out of the front window. I don't know what made me look out at that moment; I hadn't looked out the entire time we were sitting there. I saw our car parked in the front entrance area. I jumped up and said, "Lyle's here!" I pointed to our car. My bishop jumped up as well. He told the registration woman we would take care of the rest later and followed me out. Now, I knew for sure everything would be okay. Brant would be okay because my husband was here. I could hold onto him and his strength.

We didn't see him in the lobby so we went to the elevators and up to the PICU. I ran, as I got off the elevators, up to the nurse's station. My husband wasn't there. Where was he? I looked up and down the hall, then turned to the nurse and asked if she had seen my husband. I turned and looked down the corridor towards the elevators again and saw him walking quickly towards me. He was accompanied by two men, who apparently were security guards. I assumed they were there to guide him to us, and I remember thinking how kind everyone was. The doctor, nurse and our bishop stood with me. There was a third man standing near the corner of the nurse's station, another security guard. They were all watching intently, but I didn't realize nor notice their concern.

I started towards Lyle and met him a few feet away from the nurse's station. I started to sob again as he put his arms around

The power of love and gratitude will dissolve all negativity in our lives. No matter what form it has taken.
— UNKNOWN —

me. He said, "Are you okay?" I pushed my head harder into his shoulder with my arms around him and just cried. I couldn't respond; all I could do was cry. Later we learned from a nurse that it's required, in this type of circumstance, to have security there as the husband and wife see each other for the first time. She told us it's very common for them to attack one another, even physically, and blame each other. She explained they sometimes have fist fights that security is forced to break up. This is because one or both become violent, not knowing how to handle their emotions. In our case, they followed protocol and increased security. When I learned this, I was even more grateful than ever for my stalwart husband and his love for me. The nurse told the security guards they could leave. I noticed their kind dispositions as they were leaving. My thoughts were how nice it was of them to guide my husband here, not knowing at that time their real reason for being there. It's no wonder their dispositions were kind. They could leave with a pleasant spirit prevailing instead of a violent one. The nurse told us later she knew we would make it through whatever happened when she saw my husband's first concern was for me. She said it really touched her.

Dr. McCarthy again explained, this time to Lyle, what they had done and were doing with Brant. He explained the bolt they had, by this time, placed in Brant's head. He shared Brant's prognosis which was his heart was beating on its own but his breathing was being maintained by a ventilator and Brant was in a coma. "However," he said, "As bad as it is, you just never know." Then he told us we could go see Brant.

If we were logical, the future would be bleak indeed. But we are more than logical. We are human beings, and we have faith, and we have hope.

— JACQUES COUSTEAU —

Treasure the Memories

$\mathcal{A}$s we walked in the room, I wondered how this could be possible. When we got up this morning, it was just another normal day, maybe a little more hectic than usual, but still normal. Brant had started climbing out of his crib about a month earlier, at the age of fifteen months. We had his crib at the very lowest place it could be set at, but nothing stopped him. He was a big boy for sixteen months. He was bigger at this point than any of his three older brothers had been.

As you fall asleep at night take a minute to think back over the day. Remember the moments that were wonderful, and give thanks for each one of them.
— UNKNOWN —

I would usually be in the kitchen making breakfast for our school-age children when I would hear him start to stir. Our house was about 2800 square feet on the main level, and the kitchen was on the opposite side of the house from Brant's bedroom. I would always try to reach him before he climbed out, fearing he would fall, but he was just too quick. I usually made it to the opposite end of the hallway as he would walk out of his room. We had developed a little ritual. I would crouch down to his level and, while holding my arms out to him, say "Brant!" He would respond with "Mommy-e-e," as he ran and jumped in my arms. I would hug him and cover his face with kisses while I swayed back and forth.

We'd had our ritual just a few hours ago—only just a few hours before he was running into my arms. How was it possible he was now lying in this hospital bed, with tubes and monitors everywhere? There was even a bolt in the top of his head where he once had a curl. It was a natural curl, and it didn't matter what I did, it would not stay down. I called it his Cupid doll curl. It was a perfect curl all the time, and now it was gone.

> We all have disappointments and discouragements—that is part of life. But if we will have faith, our setbacks will be but a moment and success will come out of our seeming failures. Our Heavenly Father can accomplish miracles through each of us if we will but place our confidence and trust in Him.
> — Ezra Taft Benson —

Years later, I wondered why I didn't ask the nurse for the hair they cut off. At the time, I was afraid . . . I'm not sure why or of what. I developed phobias during this experience; phobias I had never had before. Eventually I overcame them, but not without an effort on my part. It began with the curl. I think I was afraid if I asked for it, it was some kind of an omen that he would die. I wouldn't let anyone take pictures of him while he was in the hospital either. It was the same fear, and I was consciously aware of it. I felt if I allowed pictures to be taken, it meant I didn't have enough faith, and I was accepting he could die. I was so confused; I didn't understand that one had nothing to do with the other. Consequently we lost some very precious moments in pictures with our son.

The feeling in Brant's room, although solemn, was also hopeful. It was definitely a reality check. Life is so fragile. Our loved ones are so precious. What else is there in life?

I walked over and stood on the right side of Brant's bed. There was a small chair near it. Someone, I think it was our bishop, pulled it up for me to sit down. I was pregnant and had not eaten all day. I felt weary and overwhelmed. Needless to say, I felt very grateful for a chair. I sat down and took my little son's hand in mine. My husband was standing on the other side of Brant's bed and wanted to give Brant another blessing. As he and my bishop did so, I again prayed in my heart to my Father in Heaven to please leave my son here. All I could do is beg over and over in my mind. The nurse asked me if I would like to hold Brant, but I told her no. Again I was having the same fears, that if I held him I would be admitting he may die. And I was determined I wouldn't show any signs of a lack of faith . . . very foolish. She said that if I changed my mind to just let her know. I thanked her, and she left us alone.

> *Yea, though I walk through the valley of the shadow of death, I will fear no evil: for thou art with me; thy rod and thy staff they comfort me.*
> — PSALMS 23:4 —

I don't know how long our bishop stayed, nor am I completely sure who of our family arrived first. I did get word my sister had our children. My mother's brother, my Uncle Ken, was one of the first to arrive at the hospital. I'm very close to my Uncle Ken, and he offered so much support. I was informed that my mother and father had been contacted, and they were on their way.

Over the next five days we had family from both sides with us almost nonstop. Even my eighty-year-old Grandma Leavitt was with us nearly every day. Everyone gave us so much support and hope for our son's recovery. Even the nurses and Dr. McCarthy were so hopeful in their attitudes. Only my grandmother, who I adored, seemed less hopeful. She has an ability to receive special understanding, a sixth sense if you will, in things like this, and she didn't offer any encouragement. She had a special experience one night; her youngest daughter was killed in a car accident and came to say goodbye to her. She was awaiting the news the next day, as my uncles and aunts arrived to inform her of Twyla's death. This was one of many experiences she'd had. So when her attitude was one of wanting to prepare me for the worst, I was very upset. I wanted to believe she just didn't have enough faith. I was disappointed because I desperately needed her power and belief that Brant would recover. Most of my family just comforted me. I don't think they knew what else to do.

I began to feel I needed a place to be alone; I needed a place to pray. I found solace in the bathroom across the hall.

By Friday, the day after Brant's drowning, word had spread through our ward and stake. We even had friends bring food to us in the hospital. I hadn't eaten since the morning before, and I didn't feel hungry. I only wanted to sit by my son's side or go in the bathroom and pray. When I did pray, it wasn't a prayer, it was a pleading.

There was a room for families a few doors down the hall. We were told we could stay in there and sleep on the couches. It was large, and we could gather as a family, keeping some of the commotion out of the hallway.

By mid-morning on Friday, my husband and my mother began to worry about my condition, as well as our unborn baby's health. Together, they went to the hospital cafeteria and got me French toast. My husband was quite animated about giving it to me. In an effort to get me excited about eating it, he said, "Look what we found—French toast! We knew you'd love that!" I did love French toast, and I didn't feel I could disappoint them because Lyle was so excited, or tried to be. I took a bite. I was shocked at the taste. There was absolutely zero flavor. It was like eating cardboard. I asked them if it tasted good to them. My mother said she thought it was surprisingly good. That's why they were sure I would like it. I realized it was me, and I just couldn't eat. I didn't want to eat or sleep, I couldn't. I needed and wanted to just stay by my son.

*For where
two or three are
gathered together in my
name, there am I in
the midst of them.*

— MATTHEW 18:20 —

Cardiac Arrest

I realized I needed to change my clothes. The smell of my clothes where Brant had vomited on me the day prior as I had tried to resuscitate him, was making me really nauseous. I asked the nurse if there was some place I could take a shower. The nurse explained they didn't have that type of accommodations for parents as of yet. They were remodeling the PICU wing to improve it in that way. She went on to explain that was the reason for the remodeling and the mess. There were beds and many other items all over in the hallway. We would have to go home to shower and change. I didn't want to leave. What if Brant woke up and I wasn't there? I needed to stay; he needed to feel me nearby so he wouldn't be afraid. Lyle reassured me it would be okay. He was very concerned for me and felt it would be good for me to go home and rest a while, as well as take a shower.

Only a life lived for others is a life worthwhile.

— ALBERT EINSTEIN —

We lived about a half hour or more from the hospital, depending on if the traffic was good and the lights in our favor. I felt so guilty leaving. I thought it would be best if I got right in the shower. I would rest after, if I could. While I was in the shower, the phone rang. My heart leaped and I knew something was wrong. Lyle answered it. It was the hospital.

I jumped out of the shower and dashed into our room. Brant had gone into cardiac arrest not long after we left the hospital. They shocked his heart and started it beating again. They said he was stable, but they felt we should come back to the hospital as quickly as possible. I threw on my clothes, and we left. All I could think was, *I knew I shouldn't have left. I knew it.* I realized I needed to change, but I felt sure if I left, something would happen. I knew if I remained right by his side and watched over him, it kept him there. My desire and determination to have him stay with me was so strong. We drove quickly back to the hospital.

The lights and traffic seemed in our favor—it was as if we had angels helping us—but it still felt like it took forever. I prayed all the way there to my Heavenly Father. I know he heard my plea. He had allowed Brant's life to continue. I needed Brant to stay; I could not accept that he might die.

We met my Uncle Ken in the lobby as we went to the elevator. He informed us that prior to the cardiac arrest, Brant's condition seemed to be improving; but with his heart stopping, his condition was more critical than ever. There was an unspoken air of anxiety that surrounded my Uncle Ken. I decided I wouldn't leave Brant's side again.

Press forward, Saints,
with steadfast faith in Christ.
With hopes' bright flame
a light in heart and mind.
With love of God and love
of all mankind.
Alleluia, alleluia, alleluia!
Press forward,
feasting on the word of Christ.
Receive his name,
rejoicing in his might.
Come unto God;
find everlasting light.
Alleluia, alleluia, alleluia!
Press on, enduring in
the ways of Christ.
His love proclaim
thru days of mortal strife.
Thus saith our God:
"Ye have eternal life!"
Alleluia, alleluia, alleluia!

— Marvin K. Gardner

Our church organized a special fast, ending with a prayer, for the following morning, Saturday, at 9:00 a.m. They were holding it in the chapel we attended, near our home. The outpouring of love, support and concern was truly amazing. People we didn't even know became involved. The mother of my sister's husband asked if she could call the Christian radio station and request the fasting and prayers of those that would like to participate throughout the city. I didn't know people did things like that. I was becoming more and more

> *Ye have heard that it hath been said; thou shalt love thy neighbor, and hate thine enemy. But I say unto you, love your enemies, bless them that curse you, do good to them that hate you, and pray for them which despitefully use you, and persecute you;*
> — MATTHEW 5:43-44 —

aware of the goodness of people and how many good people there are. Sometimes the evil that happens in the world and the negative news on TV is all we hear about.

My husband asked if I would like to attend the prayer meeting in the morning. He knew my answer before he asked. I wouldn't leave Brant again. I was afraid if I did he would leave us. Lyle agreed I should stay with Brant.

Late that night, the doctor on duty, Dr. Carlisle, had the nurse wake us. I had actually managed to just fall into a deep sleep. He wanted to talk to us about Brant's prognosis. He needed to know what we wanted to do if Brant had another cardiac arrest. He explained that by law they were required to do all they could to revive the patient the first time, but after that they could let the patient go, if the family requested it. I was stunned—what was he suggesting? I looked at my husband to see his reaction. I hoped he didn't agree. Lyle was very kind but firm in his response.

"Do whatever you have to, to keep our son alive." I was relieved. The doctor's response was one of annoyance. He wasn't the warm, caring personality of Dr. McCarthy. He didn't show any compassion towards us at all. We were just his job. I thought *it's not any wonder you're the doctor at night. You're cold and uncaring.* I didn't say it to him, but I thought it. I found out later that he was actually the doctor in charge of the PICU. I surmised he must be in the position because of age, seniority or experience, because it certainly wasn't his bedside manner. We would have another encounter with this doctor later which would further reinforce my opinion. I really didn't like him, and those were feelings I didn't need or want in our circumstance.

*Being filled
with God's love is the
most joyous of all things
and is worth every cost.*

— JOHN H. GROBERG —

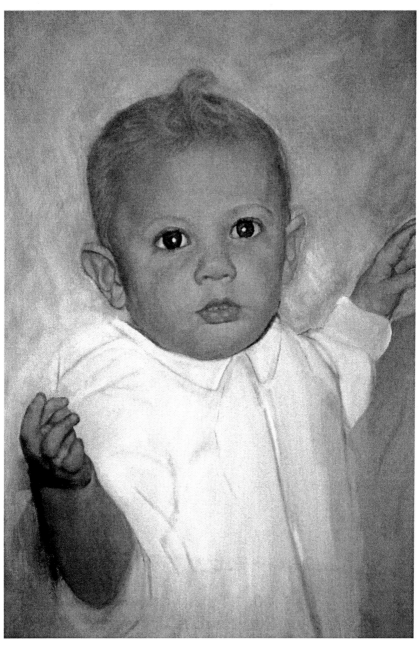

L. Brant Wood, age 6 months
Painting by Lori Wood

Brant, I Don't Want You to Go

I spent more than half that night at our son's side. Only when exhaustion took over did I give in to sleep. I finally relented and slept on the couch in the family's room for a short time. Early the next morning, I went back into Brant's room, resuming my place in the rocking chair one of the hospital staff had brought in for me. I had a very calm feeling come over me as I picked up his tiny hand. I leaned my head toward the bed and put the palm of his hand flat upon my right cheek. I put my hand over the top of his, on my face and closed my eyes. That was the closest I could get to loving and nurturing my baby.

> *Tears of gratitude come from a heart that is completely connected with the love of a caring God.*
> — UNKNOWN —

The hospital was so quiet at this early hour, and a very serene feeling prevailed. The sun was just beginning to come in through the frosted window of his room. It wasn't until after the following experience happened that I realized I had been somewhere else. I was actually in a different realm for a time. My body was still in the hospital holding Brant's hand on my face, but in my mind's eye, I was in some other place. That which I am about to share is very sacred to me. In fact, I would hesitate sharing it at all because of those who might question or doubt, but

Nearer, my God, to thee,
nearer to thee!
E'en though it be a cross
that raiseth me.
Still all my song shall be
nearer, my God, to thee.
Nearer, my God, to thee,
nearer to thee!
Though like the wanderer,
the sun gone down,
darkness be over me,
my rest a stone,
yet in my dreams I'd be
nearer, my God, to thee,
nearer, my God, to thee,
nearer to thee!
There let the way appear,
steps unto heav'n;
all that thou sendest me,
in mercy giv'n;
angels to beckon me
nearer, my God, to thee,
nearer, my God, to thee,
nearer to thee!
Then with my waking thoughts
bright with thy praise,
out of my stony griefs
Bethel I'll raise;
so by my woes to be
nearer, my God, to thee,
nearer, my God, to thee,
nearer to thee!

— SARAH F. ADAMS

for those who are willing to receive it through the spirit, they will know of its veracity. It was as real an experience as any physical experience I have ever had. It is for those that are in need of hearing it that I am willing to share this very special pearl in my life.

Whether I was in my body or out, I'm not sure. However, I know I was sitting in the same rocking chair, but I was some place other than the hospital, or at least the surroundings were different. I was sitting with Brant's palm against my cheek; my eyes were closed; my elbows were on the side rail of the bed; and my head was slightly bowed. In an instant, I was in a different realm. It was dark all around me. I didn't know where I was, nor did it matter to me. I just noticed it was dark, and the best way to explain it would be that it seemed without space. I was aware I was still in the rocking chair from the hospital, but I was sitting up, resting against the back of the chair with my hands in my lap.

A handsome young man dressed in a dark blue suit came toward me. He walked around the back side of me from left to right and stood facing me on my right side. He was standing at the side of the little body on the hospital bed facing me. He said, "Mom." I knew at once it was Brant. He was in his adult spirit. I recognized and knew him. I didn't notice the details of his face then but have since been given the vision of those details.

As I turned my head and looked up at him, I said, "Brant, I don't want you to go!"

He replied calmly and gently, yet in a very matter-of-fact attitude, "I know, and I'm willing to stay, but you need to understand it's not up to us. It's up to our Heavenly Father."

> *His gospel is the perfect prescription for all human problems and social ills. But His gospel is effective only as it is applied in our lives. Therefore, we must "feast upon the words of Christ; for behold, the words of Christ will tell us all things that we should do" (2 Nephi 32:3). Unless we do His teachings, we do not demonstrate faith in Him.*
> *— EZRA TAFT BENSON —*

"I know." The interesting thing here was that I said, "I know," but I had not really thought about that. As soon as the words were out of my mouth, I felt surprised I said what I did, and with such conviction, when it never had entered my mind that this was my Father in Heaven's decision—not mine.

As quickly as I'd entered this realm and had this experience, I was back. I felt a wave of shock come over me. I opened my eyes to see where I was. I lifted my head and looked around, surprised to find myself with my little son in the hospital room. I was so filled with the Spirit, I felt as if my heart would explode. I immediately jumped to my feet and went to find my husband. I knew what had just happened was a very special gift of the Spirit. I had heard of special out of body experiences that other people had received, but I never expected such a rare and sacred event for myself. I knew my son had been sent to give me a message.

After years of pondering this experience, I have realized how very rare and special it was. I've tried to have something like this happen again. I've prayed to have another visit from Brant, and I have had many other special experiences, but nothing that has surpassed this. As I said, it's as real of a memory as any physical occurrence I have ever had.

I ran down the hallway and could see my husband laying on one of the hospital beds, which were being stored at the end of the hallway where the remodeling was taking place. I rushed to his side and blurted out, through the tears that poured out as a result of the spirit I felt, "Brant just came to me!" He bolted up, and I could see he knew immediately it was true. He asked me what he said. I repeated our conversation, word for word, exactly as I have written it. I have never forgotten the vision or the exact words he said to me. It's as clear today as the day it happened.

Lyle then asked me something I thought was a little strange. He asked, "What was he wearing?"

"He was dressed in a suit, like a missionary," I said. "Why?" He just nodded his head as if understanding something. I again asked him, "Why?"

He shrugged his shoulders and said, "I just wondered what he would be wearing, and that makes sense."

He then jumped off the bed and said he had better go. He didn't want to be late for the prayer meeting. We walked back to Brant's room together. He put his arms around me, hugged me tight and left. The spirit was sweet and very strong as I watched him walk to the elevators. I felt my vision of Brant had been a message for him, as well as me.

But covet earnestly the best gifts: and yet show I unto you a more excellent way.
— I Corinthians 12:31 —

I sat back down by Brant and began to ponder what had just happened to me. I specifically thought about the way I responded to Brant when he gave me the message. Did I really know it was up to our Heavenly Father as I'd said? Sometimes saying we know and really believing are two very different things. The reality of checking our mind against our heart is a very hard thing to do. I knew it was up to Heavenly Father in my mind, but I had never actually turned it all over to him and trusted in the outcome. My prayers had only been pleas up to this point. Never once had I said, "Thy will be done." I had never accepted, in my heart, that the answer might be no.

The question that might come to mind, as came to mine is; how was Brant's spirit able to visit me when his body was still alive? After a great deal of study and prayer on the subject I concluded this: after the cardiac arrest on Friday, Brant's spirit didn't re-enter his body, if it even re-entered after his initial drowning. His body was being maintained by the machines, but I don't believe the doctors and their equipment were the only life support he was receiving; there was a greater power keeping Brant alive. His body was in a life-supported state as the decision was being made by a higher source. Whether that is a council or just our Heavenly Father, as Brant mentioned, wasn't important. The important point was it wasn't in our hands or the hands of the doctors. I do believe the doctors were an instrument in the Lord's hands to keep Brant alive, and they did their job very well. While his body was in this 'in-between state', Brant's spirit was capable of doing other work and he was given the right to bring this message to me.

I was left alone with my son for several hours. I learned how to read the monitors and what each number meant and where each one needed to be. His heart rate had stayed normal since the cardiac arrest the day before. His blood pressure was strong and his oxygen saturation levels were good.

To the onlooker they would think he was a sleeping child, but I could see the paleness in his face, and I knew he wasn't just sleeping.

When Lyle returned, he shared with me all that happened at the prayer meeting. He said he was so surprised and touched at how many had been fasting on Brant's behalf. Everyone met together to have a special prayer for Brant and to break their fast. They asked Lyle to brief them on Brant's condition. The word had spread about Brant's accident, and friends from past and present were there very early on this Saturday morning. It was so moving. I wondered if I would be so compassionate and charitable if it were someone else's child. I am continually amazed at the goodness in people. I am always learning and growing from their example. There are so many wonderful people I want to emulate.

> *It is not expedient for me doubtless to glory. I will come to visions and revelations of the Lord. I knew a man in Christ above fourteen years ago, (whether in the body, I cannot tell; or whether out of the body, I cannot tell: God knoweth;) such an one caught up to the third heaven.*
> — 2 CORINTHIANS 12:1-2 —

I discussed with Lyle the experience I had that morning. We talked about the message Brant was sent to give me, us, and everyone. Lyle asked if I had been praying with the understanding of "Thy will be done." I thought of my grandma Leavitt; she was trying to teach me the same thing. I grew so much in the understanding of our Father in Heaven and His ways that day. The greatness of Brant's message to me had only just begun to establish its power; a power that would enable life itself. Through the coming years this would prove to be more profound than I could ever comprehend at that time. I retreated at once to my secret place in the bathroom across the hall. I expressed my desire to have my son live. I expressed my love for him and more importantly, my love for my Heavenly Father. I then concluded with, "Whatever is Thy will . . . I will accept." My prayers continued from that time on in that same manner. I grew closer to my Heavenly Father than I had ever been. I felt encircled about in his arms.

When in the wondrous realms above our Savior had been called upon to save our worlds of sin by love, He said, "Thy will, O Lord be done."

The King of Kings left worlds of light, became the meek and lowly one; in brightest day or darkest night, He said, "Thy will, O Lord, be done."

No crown of thorns, no cruel cross could make our great Redeemer shun. He counted his own will but naught, and said, "Thy will, O Lord, be done."

We take the bread and cup this day in mem'ry of the sinless one, and pray for strength, that we may say, as he, "Thy will, O Lord, be done."

— FRANK I. KOOYMAN

Blessing? Trial? Or Both?

A friend of mine from high school heard about Brant's accident. She came to visit that day. I think she was on a mission. She could see my determination and desire to have faith at all times that Brant would live. A friend of her's had a son that survived a drowning accident. He was left without any capabilities at all. He was always in a critical care state. They had to have twenty-four hour care for him at all times, and he was at home. They had been caring for him for several years under very difficult circumstances. She said that she hurt for the family. She felt the other children always came second; there wasn't any other choice. They couldn't go places as a family. Their lifestyle was completely altered.

These things I have spoken unto you, that in me ye might have peace. In the world ye shall have tribulation: but be of good cheer; I have overcome the world.
— John 16:33 —

She looked at me in an almost cold way as she said, "Lori, do you want to live like that?" I wondered why she'd come. What was she trying to accomplish here?

I looked back at her just as determined and firmly said, "Yes, I don't care; I just don't want to lose him. I'll take him any way I have to. I'll do whatever I have to." I could tell she was disappointed at my response.

I knew she didn't understand; nobody understood. I didn't care what they thought. They couldn't possibly know what I was feeling, how my heart ached.

My friend only stayed a short time, just long enough to tell me this story. At the time I wished she hadn't bothered coming at all. I didn't feel comforted by her visit; I was only left empty and a little angry. Later, years later, I understood what she was trying to help me understand. It took me many years, but I finally appreciated her visit to me. As I look back, I know it wasn't easy for her. I'm sure that is why I didn't feel a warm feeling coming from her. What she was trying to say was hard and had to be said in a matter-of-fact manner, without emotion. It ended up being very good for me. I probably never even thanked her; I hope she feels my gratitude today.

> *And to all who suffer—to all who feel discouraged, worried, or lonely— I say with love and deep concern for you, never give in. Never surrender. Never allow despair to overcome your spirit. Embrace and rely upon the Hope of Israel, for the love of the Son of God pierces all darkness, softens all sorrow, and gladdens every heart.*
> — Dieter F. Uchtdorf —

I would like to interject something here. I am not suggesting that when people are given challenges such as special needs children, or children that are in need of constant medical care, that it is a negative in their lives. I think it is, more often than not, quite the contrary. I've had the opportunity to watch several families take on these great challenges, only to have their families grow and become even stronger. I believe they wouldn't be the same without their "special children."

Later that afternoon, my Uncle Ken came to see us again. He stayed at the hospital a long time. He is such a loving man; he always lifts my spirit.

He's just one of those people that have a way of warming you. I think he was probably the last one to leave that night; he stayed even past my mother. He was very troubled because he and his wife were leaving town the next day. They had scheduled a cruise months before and had to be there the following night. I was sad he was leaving but assured him all would be well, and that I would be fine. The next day, Sunday, early in the morning, my uncle dropped in again to say good-bye. Everyone showed so much love and concern, but there wasn't anyone, outside of our parents, that was equal to my uncle.

Lyle's parents had come as well, to stay in our home and help my mother with our children if she needed it. I was glad to have them there. Lyle's sister, who lived in Florida, had flown out to be with us too. There were so many that sacrificed so much on our behalf.

In the family's room there was a television, which we turned on to keep us company from time to time. It helped reduce the anxiety that bore down upon us. During this time, there were "special news breaks" occurring continually because an older man in a wheel chair had apparently been pushed overboard on a ship named the "Aquili Laurel." I don't remember the what's or why's, I just remember it was constantly on the news on every channel. I thought to myself, *the whole country is aware and upset over the death of this aged man while my little son is lying at death's door, and very few even know! The world is traumatized over one man, but would they shed a tear for Brant if he died?*

It seemed so out of proportion to me. I realized people cry everyday at the loss of loved ones, and many were probably crying, as I was, for

> *When frustration and impatience challenge charity, hope braces our resolve and urges us to care for our fellow men even without expectation of reward.*
> — Dieter F. Uchtdorf —

their child right then. I wondered if the incident with the man was just a little over dramatized. Or maybe the world's concern for him was a concern for anyone who was in pain, which they might not know of, and it was just focused through this man. Or perhaps he was famous or wealthy and, therefore, he was known by everyone. Does that make it understandable? I do admit, at the time, it didn't seem fair or under-standable.

I know that Heavenly Father will receive one with the same love as the other, if they've lived their lives in a way to be welcomed with open arms. It doesn't matter how obscure and unnoticed your life or death may be to the world; it's what you've done with that life that gives you place in His heart. He is not a "respecter of persons." Those were the thoughts that penetrated me to my very core at that time and have returned to my mind with profoundness many times since.

Search diligently, pray always, and be believing, and all things shall work together for your good.
— Doctrine & Covenants 90:24 —

My Heart Broke For My Children

As the day lingered on, our family came and went but not as many as the two days prior. My mother had informed me earlier that our children wanted to see Brant. I said no because I was concerned it would disturb them too much to see him this way. I felt it would be best to wait a while, at least until he re-

> *Faith is not so much something we believe; faith is something we live.*
> — JOSEPH B. WIRTHLIN —

covered a little. But today, as Lyle and I talked, we felt that it may not be wise to wait any longer to let them see their brother. Lyle was especially concerned and aware that if Brant didn't live, our children wouldn't have had an opportunity to say goodbye. I didn't want to think that this might be a reason to have them come, but I needed to be logical and accept the possibility of it.

I called my sister's home where my mother was staying at that time because my sister still had our children with her. I asked if she and my father would bring our children to the hospital. It was Sunday afternoon, and as they had already attended church that morning, it was a good time for them to come. I hadn't seen our children in three days, and I really missed them. I was worried about them, especially Kyle. He was so little himself, and I was concerned about the trauma he had been through.

I need thee every hour,
most gracious Lord.
No tender voice like thine,
can peace afford.

I need thee every hour;
stay thou near-by.
Temptations lose their power
when thou art nigh.

I need thee every hour,
in joy or pain.
Come quickly and abide,
or life is vain.

I need thee every hour,
most Holy one.
Oh, make me thine indeed,
thou blessed Son!

I need thee, oh I need thee;
every hour I need thee!
Oh, bless me now, my Savior;
I come to thee!

— Annie S. Hawks

My mother and father brought our children to Brant's room. They were all very solemn as they walked in. I could see by their faces it was not at all what they had expected to see. The last time they saw their brother, he was vivacious and full of energy. Now he was lying in a cold hospital room in a coma with tubes and wires everywhere.

I picked up Kyle and held him. He laid his head on my shoulder and just looked at his brother. Darci put her arms around me and started to cry. Courtney and Matthew stood at the end of his bed and stared, looking very confused. Darci, who was a very mature eleven-year-old at the time, told me later she thought because they were coming to see Brant that meant he was okay. They expected to walk in and see him awake and well. They weren't at all prepared for what they saw.

My heart broke for my children as I watched their pain for their baby brother, who they adored. I knew Kyle didn't comprehend what was happening, and I'm not sure Courtney or Matt had a real grasp on it either. Darci, on the other hand, understood the gravity of it all but just couldn't imagine anything but the best happening. She was such a pillar of faith and always had been.

As I was holding Kyle, he spotted two little stuffed animals at the foot of Brant's bed. They were gifts two of our friends had brought for Brant. They were very special treasures to me because they meant, "Get well soon!" One was a "Kermit the Frog," and the other was a little caramel-colored bear. We put a small family picture in the arms of the bear. Kyle was thrilled with them. It distracted him from the pain he felt. He reached out and took both and held them close.

I testify of angels, both the heavenly and the mortal kind. In doing so I am testifying that God never leaves us alone, never leaves us unaided in the challenges that we face. "Nor will He, so long as time shall last, or the earth shall stand, or there shall be one man (or women or child) upon the face thereof to be saved."
— JEFFREY R. HOLLAND —

Our other two boys became curious with the tubes and equipment so we explained as simply as possible why Brant was asleep and also what everything was that was attached to him. I could see they were becoming uncomfortable with it all because they were beginning to get agitated and bother the machines. I knew it was time for them to go. I told Kyle that Brant wanted him to have the bear, and Brant would keep the frog. This thrilled Kyle. He gladly gave up Kermit and held the bear tight.

We walked to the elevator with my parents and our children. Although they missed us and wanted us to be at home, they didn't say a word or complain, not even little Kyle. They just obediently kissed and hugged us and entered the elevator with their grandparents. The fact that they were going to my sister's helped because her children were near their ages. My parents were so sweet and nurturing towards them, especially my father, who had always seemed a little gruff to them. I was glad they were seeing a side of him they had never really known before.

Savior, may I learn to love thee,
walk the path that thou hast shown,
pause to help and lift another,
finding strength beyond my own.
Savior may I learn to love thee—
Lord, I would follow thee.
Who am I to judge another
when I walk imperfectly?
In the quiet heart is hidden sorrow
that the eye can't see.
Who am I to judge another?
Lord, I would follow thee.

I would be my brother's keeper;
I would learn the healer's art.
To the wounded and the weary
I would show a gentle heart.
I would be my brother's keeper—
Lord, I would follow thee.

Savior, may I love my brother
as I know Thou lovest me,
find in thee my strength, my beacon,
for Thy servant I would be.
Savior, may I love my brother,
Lord, I would follow thee.

— SUSAN EVANS MCCLOUD

My father often covered his soft heart with a seemingly hard shield. He just didn't handle watching others' pain, so he covered it with this tough exterior. Lyle and I solemnly walked back to Brant's room.

Sunday slipped away without a change in Brant's condition. Family and friends were coming a little less often, which was good in some ways. Although I loved their support and wanted them there, it could get a little disruptive at times with my large family, and I felt this distracted from the spirit. I felt we desperately needed the spirit at all times if we were to have Brant recover. Although at this point I was very submissive to what the Lord would decide, I still believed we needed to have time to intently ponder and pray. This was my thought process then, and it is the same now. Lyle's parents and sister, Dorothy, were with us the rest of the evening. It was so good to have them there. They all carried a quiet strength about them, and that is a very comforting thing to feel.

They left the hospital late evening, and we were again left alone with the TV news and the man in the wheelchair who was pushed off the freighter ship. I was so very tired. At last, maybe, I could sleep a little.

I don't have a message. My message is my life.

— GANDHI —

Do You Still Want to Revive Him?

J had just fallen sound asleep—that kind of sleep that I longed for during this painful circumstance—when the doctor on the night shift, Dr. Carlisle, awakened us. He was the doctor in charge of the PICU, the cold emotionless one. I kept wondering why he would choose pediatric intensive care. He wanted to talk to us. My heart was pounding, having been awakened like that. He

> *Today I will feel love and immense gratitude for those people who are challenging me in my life. And I know my love and gratitude will dissolve all negativity.*
> — UNKNOWN —

led us down the hall, just past the nurse's station and kitty-corner from Brant's room, to an X-ray light. The light was on, and Brant's X-rays were hanging from the clip at the top. He wanted to show us the seriousness of Brant's condition. It was as if he were trying to beat it into us—as if we weren't already spending every waking moment, night and day, with our comatose son. We were very aware of the gravity of his situation.

I think back now and realize he was suggesting, without actually saying it, that we take him off life support. However at the time, we were completely oblivious to his vague suggestion. I'm sure he understood— and we didn't—all the ramifications of Brant's condition.

Truth reflects upon our senses;
gospel light reveals to some.
If there still should be offenses,
woe to them by whom they come!
Judge not, that ye be not judged,
was the counsel Jesus gave;
measure given, large or grudged,
just the same you must receive.
Jesus said, "Be meek and lowly,"
for 'tis high to be a judge;
if I would be pure and holy,
I must love without a grudge.
It requires a constant labor
all His precepts to obey.
If I truly love my neighbor,
I am in the narrow way.
Once I said unto another,
"In thine eye there is a mote;
if thou art a friend, a brother,
hold, and let me pull it out."
But I could not see it fairly,
for my sight was very dim.
When I came to search more clearly,
in mine eye there was a beam.
Blessed Savior, thou wilt guide us,
till we reach that blissful shore
where the angels wait to join us
in thy praise forever more.

— Eliza R. Snow

We would be living with our child who would never be what he had been before, our child who would probably be brain dead the rest of his life. He was saying the same thing my friend had said the day before. My feelings were the same towards him as it had been to my friend—it wasn't their child, and they just didn't understand.

They didn't understand, and yet on the other hand, neither did we. We weren't thinking of the ramifications on our family, and there would be ramifications either way it went. Our family would deal with and would always be taking care of an invalid child in constant critical condition. Or our family would deal with the loss of a family member and his absence. I'm not sure, to this day, if one way is worse than the other. I can only be grateful I'm not the one that makes that decision. That comes from a loving Heavenly Father who knows the beginning from the end. He knows, although painful, ultimately what is best for us, both individually as well as collectively.

Lyle and I stood blankly staring at Dr. Carlisle. Maybe he meant well, or maybe he just didn't want to be bothered with this critically ill child. Then he started talking about drowning. I could tell he was bothered as he began rambling about statistics and the danger of pools. All I could do was listen. I didn't want to comment or even react to what he was saying. I wondered, *is he blaming me?* He was certainly going that direction. I knew what had happened, and it had never entered my mind I might be blamed for Brant's condition. I knew I watched over my children as much or more than any mother would. I knew how close I kept them to me. How could this man, who didn't know me or know the circumstance surrounding Brant's accident, even go there? I was already in so much pain. I chalked it up at this point in time to the fact the man was just a jerk. I no longer think he was a jerk, just someone who lacked the spirit of compassion and understanding.

We politely thanked Dr. Carlisle and assured him we understood. We asked him what more could be done for our son. He assured us all that was possible to do was being done. He then once again asked if we wanted to revive Brant if he had another cardiac arrest. We pointedly and emphatically said, "Most definitely."

> *Be strong and of a good courage; be not afraid, neither be thou dismayed: for the Lord thy God is with thee whithersoever thou goest.*
> — JOSHUA 1:9 —

He looked at us in a seemingly annoyed way. I felt his eyes were saying, "You stupid fools, you just don't know what you're saying."

I hope our eyes said back, "Yes, yes we do!" We turned and left him standing there. He watched us as we went into our son's room. I was so tired, and I knew Lyle was too, but we needed to comfort ourselves with our baby's presence. He was so far away, and yet he was right there. *Oh Brant, please come back to us.*

The feeling in Brant's room was so beautiful. It's hard to describe the comfort everyone felt as they went in there. I'm not sure how long we spent with Brant that night. We finally went back into the family's room and let sleep take over again for a while.

*The brighter
our hope, the greater
our faith. The stronger
our hope, the purer
our charity.*
— Dieter F. Uchtdorf —

Do You Know What Accident Means?

On Monday morning, I had been with Brant since before dawn and got up to go pray and walk a little. As I left Brant's room, I looked toward the elevator, and my Uncle Ken was walking toward me. I was shocked to see him. I hurried to him and asked, "What are you doing here? You should be on your cruise right now."

> *I challenge every one of you who can hear me, to rise to the divinity within you. Do we really realize what it means to be a child of God, to have within us something of the divine nature?*
> — GORDON B. HINCKLEY —

He gave me a very tender hug and then said, "I just couldn't leave. I can go on a cruise anytime. I just felt I needed to stay here right now." I started to cry. So many had given up and done so much for us.

If ever there were acts of charity—the pure love of Christ—shown, it was certainly in its greatest form now, towards us. I didn't know how to even express my gratitude to everyone who had already sacrificed so much: my mother, who had flown in from Oregon and was here within hours of the accident; my father, who had dropped his trailer and immediately headed back down from Idaho where he had gone to pick up a load; my husband's parents, who left their businesses in Utah to be cared for by employees; my sister-in-law, who left her two young children and flew in from Florida; and now my dear uncle who dropped his vacation with his sweet wife, who agreed he should stay; and so many others. I was so glad my uncle was there. He stayed almost all day with us. He left only once to take care of some business he needed to attend to. My mother and dad, Lyle's sister, and his mother and dad were also with us that entire day.

> The things we hope for lead us to faith, while the things we hope in lead us to charity. The three qualities—faith, hope, and charity—working together, grounded on the truth and light of the restored gospel of Jesus Christ, lead us to abound in good works.
> — DIETER F. UCHTDORF —

At one point, everyone was gathered in the family's room while I had been in with Brant. It was early afternoon, and I was feeling especially helpless and emotional. I had eaten very little and had slept even less for nearly five days now. I got up and left Brant's room feeling completely overwhelmed. Dr. McCarthy came through the double doors that separated the PICU from the end of the hall where the remodeling was taking place. Usually these doors were propped open, but today they were closed. He came through the doors as I was walking out of Brant's room towards them. He could see my emotion. I looked at him and felt his compassion for us and our situation. Never once had there been anything but love and concern from him towards us and our little son.

As I looked at him and felt this charitable love, I broke down almost to hysteria. I didn't say anything; I was too emotional to speak. I felt tired and weak in my spirit as well as my body. He put his arms around me in a kind and gentle way. Then he stepped back and looked at me and began to talk. He didn't feel like a doctor, he felt like a good friend.

He asked how far along I was in my pregnancy. I told him I was about three months. Then he instructed me that I needed to eat. I said, "I know, but I'm not hungry."

He replied with, "That doesn't matter, you still need to eat!" He was very firm, yet kind and compassionate. He reminded me I needed to care for myself and my unborn baby. He told me they were doing everything for Brant that could be done, and I needed to go lie down and rest. He continued admonishing me, saying my body needed rest and nourishment for the sake of my baby. I nodded my head that I agreed. I knew he was right, and his concern warmed me.

I was so grateful he was the doctor taking care of Brant during the day. I had a great deal of confidence in his ability. I knew he was guided by and listened to the Spirit. The spirit coming through him was sweet and full of knowledge. He gave me a message I've always remembered and treasured. His proverb of truth strengthened me then and has offered me strength and wisdom through the years.

> On occasions, global or personal, we may feel we are distanced from God, shut out from heaven, lost, alone in dark and dreary places. Often enough that distress can be of our own making, but even then the Father of us all is watching and assisting. And always there are those angels who come and go all around us, seen and unseen, known and unknown, mortal and immortal.
> — JEFFREY R. HOLLAND —

"You do understand this was an accident." He said this with such sureness and kindness as he continued, "Do you know what accident means? It means it was not caused by anyone. No one made this happen. It was accidental."

He then went a different direction that surprised me. "I know you are a very religious person." I nodded in agreement. "Then you believe it could be God's plan to take your son at this time. Therefore, He would need a way to take him." What he said next took me off guard and really caused me to think. "Don't you think," he said, "that it's better that He would take him in this way rather than in another way that might be traumatic for someone else?"

Seeing I was confused, he went on. "For example, He could have run into the road and been hit by a car. That would have put the guilt on someone else."

I understood. Dr. McCarthy was saying if it is Heavenly Father's plan to take Brant from this mortal existence, Heavenly Father would need a way, and it didn't necessarily matter how. Wasn't it better that it happened in this way; rather than involve some other person that could cause guilt and pain the rest of their life?

> *Has the day of miracles ceased? Or have angels ceased to appear unto the children of men? Or has He withheld the power of the Holy Ghost from them? Or will He, so long as time shall last, or the earth shall stand, or there shall be one man upon the face thereof to be saved? Behold I say unto you, Nay; for . . . it is by faith that angels appear and minister unto men . . .*
> — MORONI 7:35-37 —

What a profound thought to live by; the unforeseen happens, and then we go on living, looking for the positive in the situation we're in and then doing the best we can.

I definitely felt he was sent with that message, at that moment, for me. He was not just another doctor—he was a pediatric intensive care doctor. He had seen so much. He had compassion on me, and he felt prompted to open his mouth right at a moment I would receive and appreciate what he said. I thanked him and told him I understood.

I then asked him something that had been troubling me since the accident happened. I asked, "Is it painful to drown." I was so concerned about the feelings of my son. I wondered if he had suffered. Had he been wondering where his mother was and why she wasn't there to help him? What was Brant thinking? Was he thinking, "Where is my mom?" He always counted on me being there. I know he was just a baby, but I believe he still understood these things. It was so important for my children to feel I would be there anytime they needed me, especially my babies. In my mind I would see Brant struggling under the water; I imagined this over and over. Everyone thought I was overly worried about this, but I just couldn't help it. I wanted to know from a professional if my baby had suffered.

His answer was so comforting. He said drowning was the most painless way someone could go. He went on to say that Brant

Oh say, what is truth?
'Tis the fairest gem
that the riches for worlds
can produce,
and priceless the value
of truth will be when,
the proud monarch's
costliest diadem is
counted but dross and refuse.
Yes, say, what is truth?
'Tis the brightest prize
to which mortals or Gods
can aspire.
Go search in the depths
where it glittering lies,
or ascend in pursuit
to the loftiest skies:
'Tis an aim for the noblest desire.
The scepter may fall
from the despot's grasp,
when with winds of stern
justice he copes.
But the pillar of truth
will endure to the last,
and its firm rooted bulwarks
outstand the rude blast,
and the wreck of the
fell tyrant's hopes.
Then say, what is truth?
'Tis the last and the first,
for the limits of time it steps o'er.
Tho the heavens depart
and the earth's fountains burst,
truth, the sum of existence,
will weather the worst,
eternal, unchanged, evermore.

— JOHN JAQUES

had probably blacked out almost immediately. I was so worried about how scared he might have been during suffocation. Dr. McCarthy said that he would not have felt it at all. He explained he would have blacked out, and then soon after his heart would have stopped. As morbid as this was to know, it gave me so much comfort to understand all of the medical functions. I thanked him through my tears. He put his hand on my shoulder in a caring gesture and suggested I go rest.

I walked into the family's room where my husband was. I was very anxious to share all of this with him. I could tell it offered the same comfort to him, even Dr. McCarthy's insight on the reason for Brant's accident.

At the time Dr. McCarthy shared this, it was very helpful in my understanding of God's plan for us, but it doesn't come close to what I have gained through the years since. I don't know if Dr. McCarthy really knew what he was saying, or if it was one of those moments you open your mouth and something profound comes out. And then you walk away saying, "Wow, where did that come from?" I know Dr. McCarthy was not the same religion we are, not that it matters at all, but sometimes, it just feels good to know we all get inspiration from the same source. At any rate, as I've learned, and then look back and learn more, the words he shared I believe are far more profound than either of us realized at the time. I know I have pondered this a lot, as well as shared it with many others in similar situations, and I know it has given as much comfort to them as it did me, at the time. Yes, there are angels among us.

Peace I leave with you, my peace I give unto you: not as the world giveth, give I unto you. Let not your heart be troubled, neither let it be afraid.
— JOHN 14:27 —

Brant's Blood Pressure Was Dropping

*T*he feeling at this time with everyone who entered Brant's room was *he's going to make it.* Although his condition had not changed, he had not improved, you could see the hope in all their eyes. Even the nurse that was on duty most of the time expressed her confidence in his recovery.

> *A grateful person is thankful under all circumstances.*
>
> — UNKNOWN —

Our daughter, Darci, was invited to stay that Monday night with a family from our church. I know they thought it would help relieve the pressure by taking her for the night, but I wanted to keep my children together in our home. Darci, however, has a very determined personality. She didn't understand my concerns and just wanted to be with her friend. I finally gave in, going against the feeling I had inside screaming not to let her go.

Everything seemed to be going so well with Brant. Everyone felt comfortable with his stability. Lyle's sister decided to fly back to Florida; she needed to get back to her children. There was such strength in his room. To put it simply, it was *amazing* to walk in. He was surrounded, no doubt, by angels.

Dorothy was able to get a flight that evening. Lyle's father had driven their car back home, and his mother was without a car and had our boys. That left only Lyle to take Dorothy to the airport. I didn't want him to leave, but it was the only solution.

May we learn what we should learn, do what we should do, and be what we should be. By so doing, the blessings of heaven will attend. We will know that we are not alone.
— Thomas S. Monson —

My parents and Uncle Ken had gone home for the night and I was again left alone for a couple of hours with my son. I sat down on the rocking chair by his bed. As I had done so many times in the last couple of days, I took his small, chubby hand in mine.

I hadn't been sitting there long when I had a strange anxiety come over me. It was one of those warning feelings. It was like the feeling you get when you know something is about to happen, but you don't know what. As the feeling continued to get stronger, I became nervous. I kept watching the monitors. Brant's blood pressure seemed to be dropping a little. I had the same lonely, helpless feeling I had in the first hospital where Brant was taken, when I was alone in the small room of the ER. I wanted my husband to be there. I kept watching the clock. *Please hurry,* I thought.

As I sat watching the monitors, there wasn't any question; his blood pressure was going slowly but steadily down. I looked out the window by the door of his room, to the nurse's station. I could see out the window without standing up. The night nurse was now on. She was very young and someone I had never seen before. This didn't help my confidence level at all. I hadn't seen the doctor in hours. I knew Dr. McCarthy was gone, and Dr. Carlisle must be on duty now. He never seemed to check much on Brant himself; he relied more on the nurses to keep him informed.

The nurse behind the desk had her head down. She wasn't watching his monitors as the day nurse always seemed to be doing, which I knew from watching them through the window all of the time. I looked back at the monitors in the room, then again at the clock. I held Brant's hand to my face in hopes that it would help both him and me. I closed my eyes and said a silent prayer. I opened my eyes again and looked at the monitor. Brant's blood pressure had dropped a little more.

I couldn't stand it any longer; my heart felt like it would explode inside me, and I stood up. I looked out at the nurse, but she was still looking down. I walked out of Brant's room and over to the desk. The nurse was very intently working on some homework. She didn't hear me walk up. I stood there a moment, not wanting to be rude, but it was obvious she wasn't even aware I was standing there. So I finally said, "My son's blood pressure is really dropping."

> Be one who nurtures and builds. Be one who has an understanding and a forgiving heart, who looks for the best in people. Leave people better than you found them.
> — MARVIN J. ASHTON —

She was a little startled by my voice and looked at me blankly, as if she wasn't sure what I had just said. Then she looked at the monitor for a moment. She looked back at me without any emotion or concern and said, "Okay, thank you." I walked back into Brant's room, and as I sat down, I looked over my shoulder at the nurse. She did not move, except to put her head down. She had gone right back to her homework.

I sat down and again began to watch his blood pressure drop, drop, and drop. After ten or fifteen minutes, maybe longer, I again went out and repeated my message, this time with an apparent concern and anxiety in my voice. Her response was the same as before, and she went back to her homework. I went back in Brant's room but this time stayed

How firm a foundation, ye saints of the Lord,
is laid for your faith in his excellent word!
What more can he say than to you He hath said,
who unto the Savior for refuge have fled?

In every condition—in sickness, and in health,
in poverty's vale or abounding in wealth,
at home or abroad, on the land or the sea—
as thy days may demand, so thy succor shall be.

Fear not, I am with thee; oh, be not dismayed,
for I am thy God and will still give thee aid.
I'll strengthen thee, help thee, and cause thee to stand,
upheld by my righteous, omnipotent hand.

When through the deep waters I call thee to go.
The rivers of sorrow shall not thee o'er flow,
for I will be with thee, thy troubles to bless,
and sanctify to thee thy deepest distress.

When through fiery trials thy pathway shall lie,
my grace, all sufficient, shall be thy supply.
The flame shall not hurt thee; I only design
thy dross to consume and thy gold to refine.

The soul that on Jesus hath leaned for repose
I will not, I cannot, desert to his foes;
that soul, though all hell should endeavor to shake,
I'll never, no never, no never forsake!

— Robert Keen

standing up. I kept turning and watching her and then looking at the monitor. His blood pressure continued to drop.

When it got to be about 50 over 30, I went out in a panic and said, "My son's blood pressure is really low, are you sure that's okay?" She again looked at the monitor. This time she jumped up, as if she realized for the first time what I had been saying. She bolted out from behind the desk and into his room. She was clearly very upset. She looked over at the monitors as she came in, which were on the right side of his bed, then continued to the left side of his bed to check his IV's and the medicine bags that were hanging near his bed; then rushed back to the desk and picked up the phone.

By this time my husband had returned. I was so glad to see him. I explained all that had happened with Brant and the nurse. I could see the upset cross his face. What was this nurse thinking? Dr. Carlisle rushed in to check him. After a moment, he began discussing things with the nurse. Another nurse came in a few minutes later and explained to us they were going to give Brant a shot of adrenaline in hopes to bring his blood pressure up. She put the needle into his IV, and we watched.

Almost immediately, his blood pressure went back up to normal. There was relief on the nurse's face that gave him the shot, but it didn't compare to the relief on the young nurse's face. She went back to the nurse's station and stayed. The nurse that gave Brant the shot stayed in with him for a while and then also walked out. I was so excited; I felt such a relief. Surely all would be well now. I sat down, and Lyle stood on the other side of Brant's bed.

It was late now, maybe around 11:00 p.m. We watched his blood pressure with a solemn hope. It stayed up for an hour, maybe longer. I'm not sure exactly how long. However, to our disappointment, his blood pressure started to drop just as before, slowly at first, then at a regular decline. My heart sank. As it reached a low point, too dangerous to ignore, the nurse came in and said they would try another shot of adrenaline. We waited for the results as she inserted the needle into his IV. Once again, as with the first shot, his blood pressure went up to an almost normal level.

I could tell by Lyle's countenance he was not really encouraged by this. He asked me if I thought we should call our bishop. It was so late, I hated to wake him, but we knew he would want to know.

Hope in God, His goodness, and His power, refreshes us with courage during difficult challenges.
— DIETER F. UCHTDORF —

Lyle decided to call him, and he came immediately. By the time he arrived, Brant's blood pressured was dropping again. I left Brant's room. I couldn't take watching the monitors any longer.

I walked out into the hallway and stood against the window that looked in. I felt so numb, and my heart was in my throat. I almost felt as if I couldn't breathe. I just stood there, most of the time with my eyes closed. The nurse came to me and asked if I would like a chair. I told her no. I didn't want anyone to even talk to me, but I didn't tell her that. She just wanted to do anything to help. My legs ached from standing so stiff, but I didn't want to sit. I glanced in the door at Brant once, thinking I would go back in, but I was shocked to see how pale he was. I knew he was barely holding on. I couldn't bear the thought that Brant was dying. I felt so heavy I almost couldn't stand. I felt as if I was going to collapse, and yet I didn't want to sit down either.

My husband came out to get me; he said our bishop was going to give Brant a blessing. The nurse was so respectful; she closed the blinds in Brant's room and then the door. As my husband and our bishop laid their hands on his head, I closed my eyes. During the blessing, I was so lifted up spiritually. Moments earlier, I could barely stand, but now I felt strong, as if I could "handle anything that fate saw fit to give us." I had extra stamina to endure to the end. I'm not sure of all that was said in the blessing our bishop gave Brant, but I was aware he did not bless him to recover. He blessed Lyle and me, through Brant's blessing, that we would receive comfort and strength to handle whatever was the Lord's will. Then he said the startling words that gripped my heart, "I feel this is the last blessing I will give you."

As the blessing continued, I could feel many others standing all around me. I almost felt squished, like you feel in a crowded room. I wanted to open my eyes, just for a moment to see who was there, but I didn't dare. I felt it would be disrespectful to the sacred blessing being given to my son. I was sure then and after, if I had opened my eyes I would have seen angels all around me. It didn't matter though—I knew they were there. Sometimes feeling is better than seeing. The power is stronger, and you can feel the intensity greater when you see with your heart and not your eyes. I know the power I felt as I stood there; it was both overwhelming and comforting at the same time.

Jesus said, "I am the resurrection, and the life: he that believeth in me, though he were dead, yet shall he live: "And whosoever liveth and believeth in me shall never die."

— JOHN 11:25-26 —

As Bishop Creel ended the blessing, I anxiously looked up, wanting to see a change in Brant and the monitors. But nothing had changed. Brant was still pale, and his blood pressure was dangerously low. The change, however, was in the three of us. Although still heavy hearted at the situation, without a doubt there was a different feeling in the room, and everyone felt it.

Bishop Creel was disappointed he wasn't given the right to heal him. My husband told me later that was the very reason he chose not to give the blessing himself. He said he knew Bishop Creel would not try to impose his own desires in the blessing; he knew he would only say that which he was guided to say. Lyle shared with me that he feared if he had given the blessing, he would have tried to force the issue and inappropriately bless him to be healed.

We stood in the silence of the room and felt the strong bond of love—love for Brant, love for one another, love for our Savior and the Spirit He was pouring out on us. We wanted to hold onto this special moment, as long as we dared, as it might be our last. We knew, however, that Brant's situation was getting worse, so we opened the door.

There has come to you as your birthright something beautiful and sacred and divine. Never forget that. Your Eternal Father is the great Master of the universe. He rules over all, but He also will listen to your prayers as His daughter and hear you as you speak with Him. He will answer your prayers. He will not leave you alone.

— UNKNOWN —

I walked back to the place on the wall where I had previously been. I needed to think. I began to pray, just talking to my Father in Heaven. I asked for guidance, and I asked to know what His will for Brant was. Bishop Creel came out and asked if I would like to sit down. I told him no, as I had done with the nurse earlier. I knew he sensed I was praying because he gently smiled, nodded his head and squeezed my arm.

Ten or fifteen minutes passed, and the nurse walked up. She held a needle in her hand so I followed her into Brant's room. My son looked so lifeless. She solemnly walked over to Brant and said, "Well, let's try again." I had an overwhelming feeling come to me of what I needed to do. I suddenly felt so strong and sure. I hurried back out of the room to my place against the wall. I closed my eyes and bowed my head and said a silent prayer. I'm sure my lips moved because the intensity I felt about this prayer was strong. I said, "Heavenly Father, if Brant isn't supposed to live, please, don't let this shot of adrenaline work. If he is supposed to die, please take him now." I'm not sure what came over me; I only know I was sure of what I had to do. I know I felt strong with the spirit of my Savior. I said, "Amen," raised my head and rushed as fast as I could back into the room.

The nurse had just finished putting the adrenaline into the IV. I looked over at the monitor. Nothing happened. We all continued to watch . . . still, nothing. Instead of his blood pressure immediately jumping up, as it had the previous times before, this time his blood pressure continued to drop. I knew Heavenly Father had given me, as Brant's mother, the opportunity to release him. I brought him into the world, and Heavenly Father, was respectfully allowing me to let Brant go. I had asked Him to "take him now," and so He was and I knew it.

O Lord,
who lends me life,
lend me a heart replete
with thankfulness.

— SHAKESPEARE —

It's Time To Go

The nurse had asked me a couple of days before If I wanted to hold my son. I had refused at that time for the same reason as always— fear—fear that if I held him, he might die. My husband had asked a couple of times, "Wouldn't you like to hold Brant?" I told him no, as well. Now, in this moment, I knew I needed to hold him. This would be the last time I would hold him in this life, and I knew it.

Through my tears, I said to the nurse, "I want to hold my son."

She was so sweet and emphatically replied, "Of course."

She started moving tubes and IV's and equipment around as quickly as she could. Once she had him situated, she asked me to sit in the rocking chair. Then carefully, with the help of my husband, she lifted Brant up and laid him in my arms. It felt so wonderful to hold him again. I bent my head and body over him; I held him close and tight. The tender, sweetness I felt towards him seemed to flow from every part of me and I felt so connected to him. I closed my eyes and rocked him for a moment or two. I kept squeezing my arms around him and kissing his head; over and over I kissed him. He didn't respond as he had once done, but I knew he knew his mother was holding him and loved him with all of her heart; with every fiber of my being, I loved him. I regretted, oh how I regretted later that I hadn't held him more, but I was

More holiness give me,
more strivings within,
more patience in suffering,
more sorrow for sin.

More faith in my Savior,
more sense of His care,
more joy in His service,
more purpose in prayer.

More gratitude give me,
more trust in the Lord,
more pride in His glory,
more hope in His word.

More tears for His sorrows,
more pain at His grief,
more meekness in trial,
more praise for relief.

More purity give me,
more strength to o'er come,
more freedom from earth stains,
more longing for home.

More fit for the kingdom,
more used would I be,
more blessed and holy—
more, Savior, like Thee.

— Philip Paul Bliss

very grateful to have held him when I did. I didn't know if his spirit was still in his body, but one way or the other, whether he was watching me from beside or feeling from within, Brant knew how much I loved him. He knew I wanted him to stay; but he knew I understood the decision had been made that he must go. He had completed that which he came to do. I didn't think about it at the time; but later, I did think about the decision I made as I stood against that wall. After some of the pain healed, I began to accept again what I had already accepted and agreed to in those few precious moments, in which the spirit and I were one in our understanding. But, for this moment with Brant, I just held him and loved him and cradled him.

Once in a while, I would look over at the monitor. Our baby boy's heart rate was slowing down. At first there were several beats going across the screen. Now, there were maybe five, and then a few minutes later, only four. Lyle stood next to me, rubbing Brant's head or arm. Our bishop stood against the wall. No one spoke, and no one needed to speak. It would have been irreverent at that moment.

I looked again at the monitor—two beats across the screen. Dr. Carlisle whispered something to the nurse at the door. She came in and turned the monitors off. I understood what they were saying. Brant was almost gone, and it wasn't necessary to make it any harder by watching a flat line happen. I appreciated their thoughtfulness.

It was interesting, as well, that we had instructed the doctors to revive Brant if he had a cardiac arrest. He didn't leave us that way; he left slowly, as if to say, "This is goodbye." All I wanted to do now was hold my son for as long as I could, and I did. I don't know how long I held him before he actually died, but I knew in my heart it had been a substantial length of time. When the nurse came in and explained they would have to take him for a while so they could examine him for their reports, I understood. I didn't want to let him out of my arms, but I understood.

We stepped out of the room for a moment while they checked him. When we came back in, she said they were finished, and I could hold him again. As I walked over, I noticed the blood from his body was settling to his back and the back of his head due to gravity. The reality that he was gone was so hard. I didn't feel it would be the same to hold him like this, so I thanked her and told her I wouldn't hold him anymore. I just put my arms around him as he lay on the bed. They had removed all of the tubes and IV's. I asked the nurse if she could put a blanket over his body so he wouldn't be cold. I believe that was more for me, not Brant. She gently did so. We stayed in the room with him for quite a while.

After a respectful length of time, the nurse came in and said the mortuary was here and needed to take him. She was quite concerned about us being there while they did. I think she felt, for our sake, it would be best if we left first. Lyle agreed, but I didn't want to leave. He gently put his arm around me and said, "It's time to go."

*For I am
persuaded, that neither
death, nor life, nor angels, nor
principalities, nor powers, nor things
present, nor things to come, nor height,
nor depth, nor any other creature,
shall be able to separate us from
the love of God, which is in
Christ Jesus our Lord.*

— ROMANS 8:38-39 —

Did You Hear That?

*L*yle went into the family's room to get an ice chest a friend had brought a few days earlier. As we stood at the nurse's station ready to leave, the woman from the mortuary came up to offer her sympathy and assure us they would take very good care of our son's body. She was such a strange sight, it shocked me. She was a very large woman. She wore a long, black trench coat and had medium length bleached hair. I could tell it was beached because it was yellowish orange in color, like when it's been done at home and taken off too soon. The roots were grown out about an inch and were very, very dark. It was so over processed that it had a witchy appearance to it. Although she offered her sympathy and said she didn't want to rush us, I didn't feel she was sincere. She was there to get her job done, one that called her out in the middle of a cold night, and she wanted to get it done. I really didn't want to stay at that point, but it

> *Our Father which art in heaven, hallowed be thy name. Thy kingdom come. Thy will be done in earth, as it is in heaven. Give us this day our daily bread. And forgive us our debts, as we forgive our debtors. And lead us not into temptation, but deliver us from evil: for thine is the kingdom, and the power, and the glory, forever. Amen.*
> — MATTHEW 6:9-13 —

bothered me to leave my son with her. I thought, *Here it is, four o'clock in the morning, a cold October night, and this odd-looking woman comes from the mortuary to take my son from me forever.* It wasn't very comforting.

We left the hospital, a place I had not been out of in almost four days. It seemed strange. The night felt uncomfortable, like I was in a bad dream and couldn't or wouldn't ever wake up. The night air was chilly, even in the desert where we lived.

> *Never let an earthly circumstance disable you spiritually.*
> — DONALD L. HALLSTROM —

As we walked through the parking lot to our car, I stopped to look up at the window where we'd come from and left our son. It just didn't seem right to be leaving him. I wanted to run back and hold him. I wanted just one more moment, just a little more time. I knew I was being ridiculous. I'm a very rule bound person, and that would be against the rules. *What rules?* Logic and reason seemed to flee. *But,* I thought, *after that moment, I would want another moment and then another moment.* There would really never be an end to the moments. So, I turned and walked on. I kept looking back over my shoulder at the window on the third floor. I don't know what I thought I would see, or why I thought it would help, but I was drawn to look back.

My husband broke the silence and asked, "Did you hear that?"

I blankly replied, "No." The only sound was the sound of the traffic on the street. We walked on a little further. Lyle was slightly ahead of me, as I was lagging behind, not wanting to leave.

He stopped and turned and looked at me and again asked, "Did you hear that?"

Again, I said, "No." I was a little annoyed; thinking obviously he was hearing things. He stared at me, as if he didn't understand why I would be annoyed or why I didn't hear what he heard, but he didn't say anything. He just turned around and continued to walk.

We were nearly to our car, when for the third time, he turned and looked at me and very emphatically asked, "Did you hear that?"

At this point I could tell he really had heard something, and he definitely had my attention.

> *Without faith in our Heavenly Father, we cannot be successful. Faith gives us vision of what may happen, hope for the future, and optimism in our present tasks. Where faith is, we do not doubt the ultimate success of the work.*
> — EZRA TAFT BENSON —

"What? What did you hear?"

"A voice," he said. "It said, 'This will be a blessing if you will let it.'"

I was stunned, and I said to him, "What?" I wasn't hearing him right. I was angry. *How could anyone suggest my baby laying up there lifeless could be a blessing to me?*

Lyle shrugged his shoulders and said, "That's what I heard, 'this will be a blessing . . . if you'll let it.'"

I didn't want to talk any further. We were at our car, and Lyle was lifting the ice chest into the back of our four wheel drive utility vehicle.

I said, somewhat belligerently and through tears that had started to flow. "How could our son's death be a blessing to our life?"

I could tell Lyle was startled by the words he heard as well, but very calmly and patiently he said, "I don't know, that's just what I heard." There was a different spirit about him; he seemed comforted by the voice he had heard. I think about it now and realize to hear that kind of voice could only act as a comfort to the soul, as well as a message. We got in our car without saying anything more and began the long ride home.

Lyle had contacted our parents during the time I had held Brant for the last time, to let them know Brant had died. As we drove home, we noticed our other car parked in a gas station about a mile from our home. Lyle's mother was standing near it. She, in an emotional desire to see Brant, tried to drive our car to the hospital. It was having a transmission problem, and she only got a mile down the road. We stopped, and Lyle was able to fix it so she could drive it back home.

She was so sweet and so emotional. She wanted so much to see Brant again. It touched me more than I could ever express. To know you have that kind of love and concern is what gets you through and supports you at times such as this. She shared with me a couple of years later the pain she went through. She wanted desperately to take our pain from us but didn't know how. Of course no one can do that for us, except our Savior, but just knowing she had such a desire to do so, bonded us in a way nothing else could.

Lyle's mother is an artist, and at the time of Brant's death, she began a portrait of him which she gave to us when she completed it. I know the love that went into that painting and will always treasure it for that reason.

> *I know why*
> *there must be opposition*
> *in all things. Adversity, if*
> *handled correctly, can be*
> *a blessing in our lives.*
> *We can learn to love it.*
> — JOSEPH B. WIRTHLIN —

Heavenly Father Took Brant Home

*A*lthough exhausted, having been up the entire night, I still couldn't sleep. I didn't want to sleep. Every time I closed my eyes, the nightmare of Brant's drowning replayed itself in my mind. I wondered if I would ever be at peace again. I had cried so much, I didn't even have tears left. My eyes just burned and I couldn't close them to get relief. I was caught between needing sleep and yet not wanting or daring to sleep. On top of that, I was dreading the moment we would tell our children their precious baby brother wasn't coming home.

> *And He opened His mouth, and taught them, saying; blessed are the poor in spirit: for theirs is the kingdom of heaven, Blessed are they that mourn: for they shall be comforted.*
> — MATTHEW 5:2-4 —

Our oldest daughter was still at the friend's house, and it was too early to call them. Oh, how I wished I hadn't let her go. We didn't want to talk to them until we had them all together. At last, it was late enough to call. I think it was about 6 a.m. My husband called the friend's home and spoke to her parents; he explained to them the situation. They immediately offered to bring her home. By this time, our boys were up as well. They were so glad to see us and wondered what we were doing home. Lyle gently told them we would explain in a minute.

Darci came in through the front door and into the living room where we were gathered. She had a confused look on her face as she came in. She had planned to go to school from her friend's house that day and wondered why her friend's father brought her home instead. When she saw us, I could see the concern on her face, fearful of what we had to say. I sat curled up on a barrel style chair in our living room. I didn't attempt to sit on the couch with Lyle as he gathered our four children around him. I just watched from across the room. I was so completely detached and devoid of feeling.

Lyle proceeded to explain that Brant had died during the night. I could see our children just didn't understand. Lyle continued to try to explain that Heavenly Father had taken Brant back to Him. Our children all began to cry. Lyle put his arms around all of them at once and pulled them close to him. It broke my heart to watch, but of all the heart wrenching things I've ever seen or heard in my life, was the reaction of our three-year-old, Kyle. I've never heard before or since a cry like the one that came from Kyle at that moment. It was truly the most heartbroken cry you could possibly imagine. He literally wailed with a long drawn out cry. It was a pitiful sound, and there was absolutely no way to give him comfort or take away his pain.

> *Let us make our homes sanctuaries of righteousness, places of prayer, and abodes of love that we might merit the blessings that can come only from our Heavenly father. We need His guidance in our daily lives.*
> — THOMAS S. MONSON —

Kyle cried for all of us that day; it was the way we all felt. His best friend, "his little buddy," as he put it, was taken from him. He seemed to understand, even as young as he was, what this meant. I didn't think he would comprehend death, but he did. The cries of his brothers' and sister's didn't compare to his. I've always believed it was because they felt the need to comfort Kyle. They didn't worry about their own pain, in an effort to relieve Kyle of his.

It was about 7 a.m. by that time. We all sat in our living room trying to receive comfort by being together. By this time all of our children had come over to me wanting to be comforted; I'm sure they gave me far more comfort than I was able to give them.

> *And let us not be weary in well doing: for in due season we shall reap, if we faint not. As we have therefore opportunity, let us do good unto all men, especially unto them who are of the household of faith.*
> — GALATIANS 6:9-10 —

Kyle climbed on my lap and Darci sat on the floor laying her head on my knee sobbing. After our two older sons held their arms around my neck for a while and cried, they went back to the couch to cuddle up close to Lyle. I'm thankful we both had two arms so we could hold all four of children at once. There was a knock on our front door, and Lyle's mother came in from the other room and answered it. It was a neighbor from about four blocks down the street. She belonged to the same ward in our church as us and happened to have the same last name. She was about the same age and had children near the ages of ours. She came in carrying a gallon of milk. She was emotional and a bit nervous, apparently concerned about interrupting us at that very private, sensitive moment.

She began to explain her reason for being there; the news had already spread through the church of our loss. Our bishop had called a couple of people immediately to get the word out. It spread quickly to everyone. There was a network already in place to make people aware of any emergency within the ward. This was before computers and e-mail.

The news had devastated this neighbor as she had a child near Brant's age. She could only imagine the pain we were in and could hardly bear it. She said she didn't know what to do but wanted to do something. She felt anything would be good, as there isn't a wrong gesture of love and concern in a circumstance such as this.

She then began to explain. "I remembered when my grandfather died; someone brought a gallon of milk. They felt milk always seemed to be the thing you need and the thing you're out of, especially in a large family. I didn't want you to worry about going to the store for milk. You can do without other things, but if you run out of milk, you have to go and get it." She poured this explanation out as quickly as she could. I could tell she didn't want to impose but wanted to help. She wanted us to know she was there for us, and that she loved us. She was in and out of our home quickly, leaving us with the words, "I'll pray for you."

I was so touched by this act of love and kindness. Many people came, and many more sent cards, flowers, and plants. Many brought meals and offered help with our children, which we declined, so we could stay close as a family. I remember many faces and names; I don't know what kindness was done by what face and which name. However, I will never forget this woman's face and name, or the desire she had to serve our family in a moment that might be needed. She didn't let the early hour, or the thought she might be intruding stop her; she just acted upon her promptings. No, I will never forget her beautiful gesture of "the gallon of milk."

I was so exhausted from lack of sleep and emotion, I finally fell into asleep in the chair. It wasn't a comfortable position, but I was so deeply asleep I didn't care. My husband picked me up and carried me to our bed. It felt so comforting to feel his strength as he lifted me. I slept for several hours. I could hear the activity outside our room; it all seemed so distant. But as sleep lifted, the nightmare of finding Brant in the Jacuzzi crept in once again; I relived it over and over again. I forced myself to wake up so I could escape the horror of it. Now I had to face a nightmare while I was awake; the nightmare that my son was really gone and he wouldn't be coming back. A nightmare I would not wake up from.

My body was so tired, but I wanted to be with my children, so I rose and went to the kitchen where they all were. We huddled together to strengthen one another.

Reflect upon your present blessings— Not on your past misfortunes, of which all men have some.

— CHARLES DICKENS —

A Funeral to Plan

*L*yle was planning the funeral. I hadn't even thought of that. It was Tuesday afternoon, and he wanted to have it Thursday morning at 11:00. "Why do we need it so soon?" I asked. He said he just wanted to have it then. I realize now that in his mind, having it so soon would put an end to the whole ordeal, or so he thought. That was far, far from the truth.

Lyle also wanted to have Brant buried in our hometown, in southern

The way we react to adversity can be a major factor in how happy and successful we can be in life.
— JOSEPH B. WIRTHLIN —

Utah. Again I asked, "Why?" He said he'd had a dream several months earlier; we were burying someone in the St. George cemetery under an evergreen tree. Now he realized it was Brant we were burying. I didn't want to have Brant so far from me. I wanted to be able to go visit him all the time. Even though it was only a two hour drive from where we lived, we didn't get there very much. It's just so hard to travel with a large family, and I knew this wouldn't change, especially with another baby on the way. I told Lyle I wanted to bury him where we lived, but I could tell he was adamant to have it this way. I was too tired and drained emotionally to argue. I thought he must feel something to be so determined. I felt we would always live where we were now, as we were so established there and our children were extremely grounded. But I guess he did know something because a couple of years later we moved back to St. George.

The one thing I was certain I wanted was to have the mortuary where we were from take care of Brant. The funeral director and owner, Ken Metcalf, had been a long time family friend of my husband's and had become dear to me as well.

> *Because all things have contributed to your advancement, you should include all things in your gratitude.*
> — WALLACE WATTLES —

Therefore, they were the only ones I wanted to take care of my baby. We were both in agreement on this, and the call to our hometown funeral director was made. To our disappointment, because it was a different state, the embalming of Brant's body had to be done by a local mortuary—the mortuary that picked him up from the hospital. Our dear friend assured us, however, that he would be there and handle the rest. He would take care of the casket, the funeral, getting Brant dressed, and in general, all the things that mattered to me. I was so grateful to have him involved and to know my son would be in his care. It's surprising how much something like that helps with your stability in this kind of situation.

Lyle continued with the planning of the funeral. He would ask for my input, but I was so indecisive, it just didn't seem to matter to me at the time. That was very unusual for me, as I have always been very involved and opinionated in anything that concerned our children. But this time, I lost all desire to be involved. I tried to pretend that I cared, but it was all an act, and even that took a lot of effort. Lyle was a rock, however, and just pushed forward.

The funeral was arranged. The time was set for, Thursday, October 17 at 11 a.m. Other things needed attending to as well. Our boys needed clothes that were special. They had their nice clothes they wore to church, which I thought would be good enough, but Lyle wanted them dressed in a suit and tie. I felt that was a sweet gesture and showed the respect and love Lyle had for Brant. He wanted his little boys to be dressed the best they could be. We planned to go to the mall the next day to find the right attire for all our children, including Brant.

Our children had stayed home from school that day and would stay home as long as they needed to. I wanted them to feel secure, and even school just didn't seem as important as it had before. As the day went on, we began to receive calls and visitors; that night the Lang family came over. They are amazing people, and brought light, understanding and encouragement with them. They were a family that personally knew and loved Brant.

> *"For my yoke is easy, and my burden is light. (Matt. 11:30) Life is hard, but life is simple. Get on the path and never, ever give up. You never give up. You just keep on going. You don't quit, and you will make it.*
> — LAWRENCE E. CORBRIDGE —

The florist deliveries became a regular occurrence, another very sweet and pleasant surprise. I would, therefore, fight anyone that would suggest there isn't good in the world anymore. I had never really understood or known the meaning of service until now. I wondered why people cared so much about us. Many didn't know us all that well and yet the outpouring of love and service was breathtaking. I felt if I could become as all of them, and give back just a portion of what I received during the few weeks after Brant's death, I would become a bigger, greater person, even a little more like Christ. Already the words my husband received in the hospital parking lot were coming to fruition, but it would be years before I would really recognize the intent and importance of that statement. "This will be a blessing if you let it."

As the plants, flowers and cards began to pour in, I felt such a surrounding of strength. Many people shared in cards and letters their own experiences of the loss of a child and desired to share their stories to support us. I was surprised to find I wasn't alone. I guess it's normal to feel you're the only one who has ever felt this kind of pain. It was as if people came out of the woodwork and knew what we needed. The plants especially meant a lot to me. They were a living thing. It was interesting how important it became for me to care for these plants. I wanted to nurture them and talk to them. I was filled with so much love for them. I felt they were a symbol of Brant's life, and I wanted them to be a daily reminder that there is life all around us. It took me a while to understand this was what I was feeling, but the love I had for these living plants was immediate.

> *Every life has peaks and shadows and times when it seems that the birds don't sing and bells don't ring. Yet in spite of discouragement and adversity, those who are happiest seem to have a way of learning from difficult times, becoming stronger, wiser, and happier as a result.*
> — JOSEPH B. WIRTHLIN —

The day after Brant's death and the day before his funeral, we went to a nearby mall to buy the clothes we needed. It was a strange feeling to be out shopping. It didn't seem right somehow. We went at noon and ate lunch at a favorite Mexican restaurant of ours in the mall. They had become acquainted with us because we ate there on a regular basis. Needless to say, because we were there with Lyle's parents and our children who should have been in school, our waitress wanted to know what the occasion was. Everyone was silent while searching for something to say. I could see her confusion, and I didn't see why it should be a secret. I explained our son had died, and we were there to buy clothes for the funeral. I said it pretty much in those words and with a rather monotone voice.

You could cut the air with a knife. I must have sounded so matter-of-fact, when in actuality, it was the only way I could say anything without breaking down and crying. I felt as if I were on the edge of an emotional breakdown most of the time. Everyone looked at me stunned, not knowing what to say. Lyle's mother tried to give a little better explanation, which helped. I tried to fight back the tears but just couldn't, and I began to cry. Our poor waitress, who was standing next to me, didn't know what to say or do. She said something like, "Oh . . . I'm sorry." Then she turned to make a very quick exit. She came back quite composed only a few minutes later and was very sweet. She cared for us the rest of the time with the greatest of kindness and compassion. She realized my unstable emotions and was especially kind and loving towards me. The restaurant then did something much unexpected and "comped" our meal. It seemed everywhere we went people were sent to buoy us up in the most unusual of circumstances.

We finished our necessary shopping trip, finding the perfect outfit to have Brant buried in. It was a white sweater suit, with a cap to match. A cap was important as he had the small hole in the top of his

Be strong and of a good courage.
— Joshua 1:9 —

head, where the bolt had been placed. The outfit was accented with a small, decorative stitch of baby blue across the chest. It looked almost exactly like the outfit we had him blessed in. When Lyle found it and showed it to me, I was more than just thrilled, to say the least. It seemed to connect his life together—two very sacred events—the beginning and the end of his life here on earth.

We left the mall, and Lyle's parents took our children home. Lyle and I drove to the middle of the city where the mortuary was located.

Another uneasy experience I could have done without in my life was going into the mortuary, knowing my son's body was there, and wondering if he was being cared for with respect. The feeling there was strange. I don't know how else to describe it.

The man who attended to us at the mortuary was very kind and gentle. We explained we had brought clothes for our son. He thanked us and said he would take care of it for us. We hesitated a minute. I was thinking, *that's it, we're done?* Our hesitation must have implied to him that we wanted to see our son because he then asked us if we would like to see Brant. We asked him if it would be appropriate. He told us we could, but he really didn't recommend it. He said Brant was not "made-up" yet and didn't look like we would expect. He suggested that it would possibly disturb us more than help us. I really wanted to see him, but Lyle had been around bodies that were being worked on (through his business,

> One day Jesus' disciples asked Him the following question: "Who is the greatest in the kingdom of heaven?" Jesus, having summoned a little child, set him in the midst of them and said, "Verily I say unto you, except ye be converted, and become as little children, ye shall not enter into the kingdom of heaven. Whosoever therefore shall humble himself as this little child, the same is greatest in the kingdom of heaven."
> — MATTHEW 18: 2-4 —

several years before, when he sold funeral plans for 'Metcalf Mortuary') and he told the man he agreed with him.

As we left, I asked Lyle, "Why?" Through tears, I told him I wanted to see our son.

He replied, "That wasn't our son; that was our son's tabernacle of clay. His spirit, which is still living, is with us, and it would be best for both of us if we waited until his body is prepared properly for us to see him." I knew he was right, but it didn't stop my yearning to see him.

When we arrived at home, I realized we hadn't taken a diaper for Brant. I told Lyle, and I could see it bothered him, too. He asked me if I thought Brant would need it, and I told him I believed he would. We believe in the resurrection, and we also believe that we will be resurrected even as we were laid to rest. That would mean Brant would need a diaper. I was very troubled and kept talking about it; I just couldn't rest. I couldn't bear the thought that Brant wouldn't be completely dressed and prepared for the time his body would again be reunited with his spirit. Lyle felt bothered enough that he said he would take a diaper back to the mortuary. I wanted to go too, so we went back. I stayed in

If we approach adversities wisely, our hardest times can be times of greatest growth, which in turn can lead toward times of greatest happiness.
— JOSEPH B. WIRTHLIN —

the car while Lyle took it in. When he returned, he said they were very understanding and said they would make sure he was dressed exactly the way we wanted him to be. I felt relieved and content as we drove back home.

As Thursday morning came, I could not shake the dread I had in my heart. I desperately didn't want to go. I had that anxiety you feel when you're performing in some way. My heart was in my throat. We needed to be at the church where the funeral would be held at 9 a.m. That meant everyone had to be up early to be dressed in their new clothes. I was confused at why we needed to be there at that time, as the funeral wouldn't begin until 11 a.m. Lyle just said that was the instruction Ken (the funeral director from our hometown) gave me.

Lyle was so organized and took charge of everything, including all the duties that were normally mine regarding our children. When I said I didn't want to go, he gently reassured me it was important for us to do this. He said, "I promise you, it will give us comfort and peace." I knew he was right, so I proceeded to help our children get dressed, but mainly, I took what energy I had and got myself dressed.

We knew we were leaving right after Brant's funeral to go to his graveside service, which had been arranged in our hometown over a hundred miles away. So we also needed to prepare everything for the trip, as we would be spending the night. With a large family, that can be a chore in and of itself. Things went surprisingly smooth; even Kyle was very cooperative for as young as he was. I think we all had the same feelings inside.

As we got ready to leave, Lyle said he would like to take a few pictures of Brant in his casket. At first I thought that seemed morbid, but he again assured me I would be grateful later on. "Besides," he said, "I know I will want them." I again realized he was right. Later, as years passed, I realized how very right he was. Although we didn't take many pictures, they are some of my greatest treasures. I still get emotional every time I look at them, but

> Why should we mourn
> or think our lot is hard?
> 'Tis not so; all is right.
> Why should we think
> to earn a great reward
> if we now shun the fight?
> Gird up your loins;
> fresh courage take,
> our God will never us forsake;
> and soon we'll have
> this tale to tell—
> all is well! All is well!
>
> And should we die
> before our journey's through,
> happy day! All is well!
> We then are free
> from toil and sorrow, too;
> with the just we shall dwell!
> But if our lives are spared again
> to see the saints their rest obtain,
> oh, how we'll make
> this chorus swell—
> all is well! All is well!
>
> — WILLIAM CLAYTON

that's only because they remind me of how much I love my son, and that is a great positive in my life. Because I believe in life after death, it gives me one more reason to do all I can do, and live so I will be with Brant and our family when our life here on this earth is over.

We left for the church and parked in the back so we could enter the rear doors. We were a little later than planned but felt good about our arrival time, especially considering all we had to do to get prepared. Ken Metcalf was there to meet us. I was so happy to see him. He had such an amazing spirit and strength about him. He hugged us both and offered his love and sympathy. There were a few other family members already there as well, which surprised me.

Ken suggested we go and spend a little time alone with Brant, just Lyle and me. I was so anxious to see him. However, I wasn't at all expecting the feelings that would pour out when I did. When we walked into the room that had been prepared for us to spend time with Brant, my heart felt like it would break in two when I saw my son. He was slightly elevated out of his casket, so I could easily see his head and upper body immediately. He was dressed in the little white sweater suit we bought him with the cap on his head. Although the cap looked sweet, it seemed a little out of place to see it on Brant's head. I never could get him to keep a hat of any kind on his head. I thought he looked so adorable in caps, but as soon as I would place one on his head he would begin tugging at it until he got it off.

The room was quite large and usually lined with chairs. The chairs had all been removed, except for around the walls. Lyle and I walked over together, with our arms around each other. I felt such a tender closeness with my husband, more so I think than I had ever felt before. He seemed to be holding me up, but maybe we were holding each other up. I bent over Brant's head and put my hands over him. I was surprised at the stiffness of his body and the puffiness in his cheeks. I couldn't help but feel disappointed. I don't know what I was expecting—this was his lifeless body. It bothered me at first, but then my gratefulness just to see him again took over, and it didn't bother me as much anymore. He was still my baby, and I loved him so much.

> *The Lord in his wisdom does not shield anyone from grief or sadness.*
> — JOSEPH B. WIRTHLIN —

Lyle wanted to take some pictures, but I was crying so hard I wasn't sure I could. I was able to compose myself after a few moments, as I tried to remind myself how important they would be to us later. We took one of each of us with Brant and then Lyle took several of just Brant.

We wanted to make sure we could see his casket in the pictures.

It was so beautiful—white with white flocking designs on the outside of it. It had a white satin pillow lining inside. With Brant's white suit, he looked so angelic laying there. His face was a little fatter than he was normally, but even that could be overlooked because he was so beautiful.

The funeral director came in and asked if we were ready. He was concerned about us having enough time. There would never be enough time. I wanted to hold on to this moment forever. Interestingly, I hadn't wanted to come in the first place and now, maybe a half hour later, I didn't want it to end. We still had quite a while before the funeral started so I was confused and asked, "Why the rush?"

Our friend indicated that there were many people already waiting, and we really needed to get started. *Get started*, I wondered. *Get started for what?* Lyle gestured to him to go ahead, and he opened the doors to the room we were in.

Many of our family and friends started coming in to the viewing. *A viewing*—I hadn't even thought of that. I didn't know we were having a viewing; no one had talked to me about that. *Don't I have a say in this?* Although I knew a viewing was a normal and even an expected part of a funeral, I hadn't thought through the events that would be taking place. Consequently I wasn't prepared emotionally; my only thought to that point was to get through the funeral itself.

Yes, selfish and silly, I think now, but at the time I wasn't sure I was comfortable with people staring at my son. I wanted to keep him safe. They were, of course, family and dear friends, but this was my baby. I was still in a very protective mode.

> *Blessed are those who can give without remembering, and take without forgetting.*
> — ELIZABETH ASQUITH BIBESCO —

I decided to stand right next to his head. If I had to share him, I would at least stand right next to him and protect him. Besides, I just wanted to stay near him for as long as I could. After only a couple of minutes, Lyle called my name and motioned me over to him. He was standing five or six feet away from Brant's casket and towards the door. As I walked over to him he said, "You need to stand here."

I asked, "Why?"

"Because," he replied, "people want to see you."

Oh no, I thought, *I just can't bear to talk to people right now; just how much more is expected of me?* But I did.

I stood there next to my husband and greeted people. I didn't say much. A lot of people hugged me and said they were sorry, and I knew they were. It made my emotions well up even more, knowing they were sincere. That is why they were there, to show us their love and concern, and I felt it. I said, "Thank you," a lot. That was pretty much all I could say. The more people came, the more I cried.

I kept watching my son. I didn't want to lose a minute of this time. I knew these were the last moments I would have with him on this earth and I wanted to spend them just looking at him. I wanted to hold him one last time but since that wasn't possible, at least I could hold him through the arms of my heart.

A couple of my nieces, who were very young and didn't know better, were hovering over Brant out of curiosity. This concerned me. They didn't really know Brant and were more interested in someone who was dead. They reached out and touched him, as if on a dare, and then looked at each other grinning. *Where was their father?* I was looking around for him, but he was nowhere to be seen. I had started to go over to Brant to stop them when my mother walked over and scolded them. She wasn't harsh, just very appropriate, as she always had been with us when we were children. I was filled with gratitude for her, for everything she had done for me.

Watching the kids touch Brant had really bothered me and it did for a very long time. I talked with Lyle later, and he'd been bothered by it as well, but said not to worry about it. I realized I wasn't worried—I was annoyed. I knew they were just innocent children, and I loved them, but I felt it was so disrespectful to Brant. I think now that Brant would have been watching, and I am certain he found the whole thing very amusing. I'm sure he loved them so much because they were his family, and he was so happy they were there.

First, learn what we should learn.
Second, do what we should do.
Third, be what we should be.
— THOMAS S. MONSON —

At last, the people quit coming in, and I was able to go back over to my son. Our friend shut the door, and we were left alone with just our immediate and extended family. He said it was time for us to have the family prayer—the prayer that would be said before he closed and sealed the casket and we proceeded to Brant's funeral. Time was racing by, and I just didn't have enough of it right now.

We had arranged for my Uncle Ken to give the family prayer. My Uncle Ken, who would have been on a cruise right now, I was so grateful he chose to listen to the prompting and cancel his trip. He felt he would be needed at home, and he was. We really wanted him to say this special prayer for Brant and our family. I will be eternally grateful for the sacrifice Uncle Ken made for us in one of my greatest times of need. I needed him there, and I needed his comforting prayer. I don't remember all that he said in his prayer, but I do remember Uncle Ken's humble, broken-hearted attitude as he prayed for us as a family that we might understand and accept Brant's death. Most of all, I distinctly remember the feeling of warmth and love that encircled me as the prayer was uttered.

With our arms wrapped tightly around each other, Lyle, our children and I surrounded Brant's casket for a few more minutes. It was time to say goodbye and Brant's casket was closed. Our dear friend, Ken Metcalf, wheeled it out of the room we were in, down the hall and into the chapel where the funeral would be held. Lyle and I followed directly behind with our four children at our sides. Our parents and the rest of our families followed after us. As we entered the chapel, I was stunned. There were so many people there. Again, I don't know what I was expecting, but I know I didn't expect this kind of support. I was surprised at how many came to the viewing, but it was obvious the majority had not. There were probably two hundred or more people present. I was touched once again to tears and beyond. These people could not have known our sixteen-month-old son. They were there for us, and I cannot describe the feeling of love it gave me.

As we walked in, I could see on the back row on the other side of the chapel, an ex-husband of one of my aunts. I hadn't seen him in years. Our eyes met, and I read such love and compassion coming from him to me. I knew he understood my pain, as he and my aunt had also lost a child many years before. It would have been easy for him to stay home; I wasn't expecting him to be there, and I would never have known or realized he wasn't there. But there he was, and I will never forget the look in his eyes. His face stands out in my mind over any others I saw. My heart was once again warmed by him and the others at the moment I needed it.

> *We need Heavenly Father's help. Important sources of this help come though man's service to his fellowman, through prayer, and through focus on Christ.*
> — KEITH B. MCMULLIN —

The funeral was very special. The highlight for me was the talk given by our daughter, Darci. Because Brant mimicked Darci's actions from a song she performed throughout Las Vegas, as well as other cute things he did, our kids put together a routine for him. He would perform it and when he was finished he would say, "That's my show." Lyle wanted Brant's show to be shared in the funeral and knew Darci was the only one who could express the true feelings of Brant as he performed it. It was a very difficult assignment for an eleven-year-old to be given. She touched the hearts of everyone there. Needless to say, I cried through the entire funeral, but it was hard to control the convulsing sobs during Darci's talk.

When Darci was ten, she was tested by the school district, with our permission, for an advanced placement program. It was the habit of the school to send the results of the test home with the child. We, however, received a call asking us to come in and meet with the counselor. The counselor explained he wanted to personally meet with Darci's parents because she had tested genius in common sense. He said in all his years of testing youth throughout the city, he never had anyone test that high in the area of common sense. He explained to us it was his opinion that this came from the teachings at home and he wanted to meet us. We were thrilled and flattered, but we knew it was just who Darci was. It was the spirit she came to earth with. This was one of the reasons Brant adored her. He followed her around, even copying many of her physical actions.

There was one wonderful friend of ours at the funeral who we'd become acquainted with because of our children's common talents. Although they lived on the other side of the city, our paths crossed often.

This special woman had a talent for photography and became known for it within the circle we were in. She was never without her camera and shared her talent with everyone she met. She didn't stop with taking pictures of her children; she took pictures of everyone's children. Whenever she saw a "Kodak" moment, she took it. True to her character, she was at Brant's funeral with her camera. She asked permission to take pictures; she was a very kind and considerate person that way. I was glad she was there with her camera. I didn't want to worry about taking pictures after the funeral, but I knew now I would want pictures. My response to her was, "Please do."

She gathered our family and took pictures. She took candid shots, and in general, captured every moment she could after the funeral. She didn't stop there however. Later, after she had the pictures developed, she made us a beautiful fabric covered photo album and placed the pictures in it. She brought it to us shortly after the funeral. What a precious gift. It is one of my greatest treasures to this day. It will live forever and keep Brant close to me forever. The most interesting thing about this is she died of cancer not many years later. She was still so young herself. I was saddened by the loss of such a precious woman. The saying, "only the good die young" was such a truth with both her and Brant. I hope she met Brant on the other side.

*Is there a
single thing in life any
more important that
giving thanks.*

— UNKNOWN —

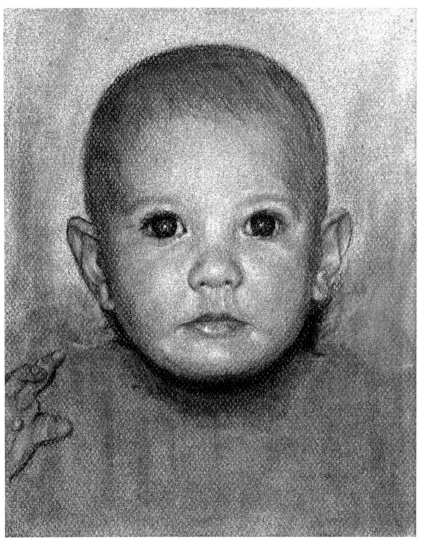

LESTER 'BRANT' WOOD   AGE 7 MONTHS   ARTIST: LORI WOOD

How Long Until It Doesn't Hurt?

*W*e traveled immediately to our hometown as the graveside service was scheduled only a couple of hours after the funeral. We had a short program planned for the graveside for those who couldn't travel to the funeral.

I can do hard things, but . . . in the strength of the Lord I can do all things.

— UNKNOWN —

It is a tradition in our church to prepare dinner for the family and close friends after a funeral, but because we didn't have much time and still needed to eat, the women in our church put together sack lunches for us. They were absolutely wonderful. They made dozens of lunches to hand out to the family as we walked out of the funeral to leave. This was just one more of the acts of kindness and charity that continued to amaze me, and once again I was touched to tears. I was so filled with love and the Spirit that it was impossible to eat at that time. We did take our lunches, though, and ate them in the car as we drove to the graveside. I noticed dozens of sack lunches still on the table as we left, but didn't think too much of it. The women in our church always prepared more than enough, and I knew they would find someone to give them to.

To my amazement, once again, when we returned home the next day, the lunches were carefully and neatly placed in our freezer in our

> *At times there appears to be no light at the tunnel's end—no dawn to break the night's darkness . . . We feel abandoned, heartbroken, alone. If you find yourself in such a situation, I plead with you to turn to our Heavenly Father in faith. He will lift you and guide you. He will not always take your afflictions from you, but He will comfort and lead you with love through whatever storm you face.*
> — THOMAS S. MONSON —

garage. Those that were serving didn't say anything to me at the time, but as I opened our freezer to get something out, there were the sack lunches. When I asked them later why they had put the food there, I was informed that they felt we would need it, and the food had been prepared so it could be frozen and used later. In fact, during that next month, I was more than once so grateful for the sack lunches in my freezer, as many times the simple task of making lunch or dinner became difficult. I was sorry to see the day when the lunches were gone, and I think our children were too.

We arrived two hours later at our hometown and went directly to the cemetery. The mortuary had several chairs set up in front of Brant's casket, which was already there and set on an elevated stand. Ken Metcalf left immediately after Brant's funeral, with the intention of arriving at the cemetery before us. That way he could have things set and ready to go. We were not too far behind him, only having stayed to have a few pictures taken by our friend and receive a few more kind words from those who had not come into the viewing.

We did get there late enough that the cemetery was already crowded with our family and friends. People we had hardly seen since high school, as well as neighbors from years prior were in attendance. In fact, there were probably seventy-five to a hundred people at the graveside. I was confused, wondering how they knew of Brant's death and the grave-side service. I learned later that the mortuary had put an obituary in the local paper about Brant. Nearly all of my friends from high school that were there had followed up as well, to make everyone aware. My husband's friends were there also, and it was the same scenario. They had spread the word amongst one another.

We were from a small town and both of us graduated from the same high school. At the time we graduated, it was the only high school in the town.

> *Don't walk in front of me, I may not follow.*
> *Don't walk behind me, I may not lead.*
> *Walk beside me and be my friend.*
> — Albert Camus —

We knew nearly everyone then, but people leave and lives get busy so I wasn't expecting to see so many familiar faces. It was so special; I didn't feel I could express the way I felt in my heart through my face or my actions. It was so hard to be responsive when I felt like I was a walking shell. My heart hurt so much, and my body was numb. I hoped people understood.

The program was short and sweet. It consisted of a prayer; a talk given by our family doctor, who was our friend, as well as the doctor who delivered Brant; a song by Lyle's brother and his wife; and lastly, the dedication of the grave, given by a close family friend. The service only lasted half an hour. Kyle, however, was so agitated prior to the graveside I didn't know what to do. Lyle's mother was so in tune. She could see he just needed a distraction from the feelings he had, which he didn't understand. Sometimes a distraction is a good thing for any age, not just a three-year-old. I wished I had learned that sooner.

There was a florist shop kitty corner from the cemetery with a balloon display in the window. Kyle was determined to go there, but I didn't know what he was looking at and why he was so determined to go. I guess I just wasn't looking. Lyle's mother came to me as the graveside service was about to begin and said she was going to take Kyle for a little walk. I felt bad that she would possibly miss the meeting, but I was relieved and grateful to her because Kyle was starting to throw a temper tantrum, and I just didn't know what to do. She took him by the hand and allowed him to lead her.

What a life lesson. She lifted our burden that day. They came walking back as the graveside ceremony ended with a balloon in Kyle's hand and a very content look on his face. What a wonderful sight it was for me to see. Lyle's mother took the time to serve a three-and-a-half year-old, who needed the service as much as any of the rest of us.

> *A man filled with the love of God,*
> *is not content with blessing his family alone,*
> *but ranges through the whole world,*
> *anxious to bless the whole human race.*
> — JOSEPH SMITH JR. —

So many of our friends that were there wanted to surround and comfort us. Once again, my sweet mother-in-law knew it was more than Kyle or our other children could deal with. They had already had a long and very emotional day for such young ones. She said she would take them home and left us to be there with our friends for as long as we needed to take. Thank goodness it didn't take too long, but a lot of comfort, which was good for both of us, did come from those precious, few moments.

There were some neighbors from our old neighborhood, which not long after we moved, had their own baby die from SIDS. They were at the cemetery, and I could hardly wait to talk to them. I didn't want to be rude to anyone else, but I was very anxious to get over to them before they left. I was surprised to see them there, as I thought it might be too much of a reminder of their own pain, which had been only a couple of years prior. But here they were, once again proof of the charity and goodness in people. I always knew that these particular friends were especially made of "pure charity."

I made my way to her, and the words rushed out, "I need to talk to you." She nodded her head, as if she already knew I would. "How long," I asked, "how long will it take until I won't hurt so much? How long will it be until the pain goes away?" I just kept asking the same thing over and over so she would understand my deep need to know.

She was patient and understanding with me but somewhat withdrawn. I understand now that her own pain was still so strong, and she was probably just trying to stay composed. She answered in a matter-of-fact tone, "A year."

"A year," I repeated.

Again, she nodded and said, "It takes at least a year until you start feeling a little bit normal again." I thanked her. She hugged me and left. I hoped she wasn't offended by my questions, but knowing now what I know, I'm sure she wasn't.

Although I had never been really close friends with her while we lived by them, I have felt a bond with her ever since, even though I have not seen her again since that day. Her words gave me comfort and hope. I felt I could survive a year. I did find that she maybe "white washed" things a little bit. Although I did feel a lot better at the year point, it was far from the end of the pain. At that point, I felt I was able to function on a more normal basis, which was probably what she meant, but the constant pain wasn't gone for a quite a while after. As a matter of fact, it never goes completely away. There is always a little tug at the heartstrings from time to time, which I feel is a good thing. It's the quiet little reminder to always be the very best you can be; never giving up when life gets you down.

I did notice at the year point that each day I began to feel better and become a little more functional. I didn't feel as if I were living in a "black hole" every single day any longer. It was at about a year after Brant's death that I laughed at something funny. My husband looked at me intently and exclaimed, "It's so good to see you smile again!" I realized that I couldn't remember smiling, even once, in the past year since Brant died. But at the year mark, I was recovering. My family was recovering, and we were beginning to live life once again.

Friends are
God's way of taking
care of us.

— UNKNOWN —

Maybe Tomorrow

*A*ll of our children had to learn to cope with their brother's death, and it was not an easy thing for any of them.

Our second son and third born child, Matthew, was especially caught at a hard time in his life. He was in first grade at school and learning to read. He had already had a bad experience in kindergarten due to a teacher who was long past overdue for retirement. She was old, tired and just plain mean. This left its scars and now, at the beginning of first grade, a very crucial year, his baby brother dies. He was very confused because of his youth and lack of understanding of death.

> *The simple secret is this: put your trust in the Lord, do your best, then leave the rest to Him.*
> — JOSEPH B. WIRTHLIN —

He needed to read every night, and he had been doing very well. Reading together had been a special time of the day for Matt until now. Even a simple project like reading with my son now seemed overwhelming. To this day, one of my greatest heartaches is the memory of Matt's face as he would bring his book in my room and ask me to read with him. I would turn him away with the words, "Not tonight."

After several nights of this, he finally said, "But mom, I'm supposed to read!"

My answer to him was the same, "Maybe tomorrow night."

I so wish I knew then what I know now. Taking time to read with Matt would have been a healing opportunity for both of us.

It's hard to sit and read with a first grader when you're depressed and don't want to do anything—very hard. But I would do anything if I could go back—even relive the pain—and take advantage of those precious moments with Matt. I was so caught up in my own grief, I didn't see the pain of my son. I eventually did read again with Matt, as did others in the family, but not until irreversible ground was lost.

We eventually put Matt in home school, which was a wonderful opportunity for both us. He was able to catch up, if you will, the lost ground of his schooling because of those painful years, but you can never take time back. It's important to live every moment you can in the moment you are in, right now.

Stresses in our lives come regardless of our circumstances. We must deal with them the best we can. But we should not let them get in the way of what is most important—and what is most important almost always involves the people around us. Often we assume that they must know how much we love them. But we should never assume; we should let them know.

— Thomas S. Monson —

Get Over It and Get On With Life

Sometimes more harm than good is done by those who don't have patience in the natural healing process. There are those that think they're doing you a favor by giving you a "pep" talk, however, there is a process that must be followed in any recovery. There is the feeling of loss in other things besides the death of a loved one. Divorce would be another example that would leave a feeling of loss.

STEPS FOR GRIEVING

1. Denial and Isolation
2. Anger
3. Bargaining
4. Depression
5. Acceptance

About six weeks after Brant died, the phone rang. Lyle wasn't home at the time, and I answered it. It was the man above Lyle in his business. Lyle was self-employed but worked within a matrix in the life insurance business. I explained to him that Lyle was gone, and he asked me how he was doing. I responded in as supportive and positive a manner I possibly could. I felt very uncomfortable, as if I were being questioned in an attacking manner. It put me in a very defensive mode for my husband. I tried to explain how hard it is to feel motivated to talk to people about life insurance when your son just died six weeks ago.

His response to me was, "Well, you just need to tell him it's time to get over it and get on with life!"

I said, "Okay, goodbye," and hung up. I'm not sure I even gave him a chance to say goodbye. I know I didn't hear him respond I hung up so fast. I was hurt and angry. *How could he be so unsympathetic and judgmental?*

I expected so much more from him.

He had been very successful in business—he was worth millions—and it had changed him. His attitude was nothing gets in the way of success in your business, and that success was measured by how much money you made—period. He used General Patton as his theme in every meeting he held, and his attitude was "no slack."

The general demeanor in his voice had come through the phone loud and clear. My anger then turned to tears, and I realized some people just don't get it. They choose not to. After many experiences in life, I eventually began to feel sorry for this man. Although we didn't have the money he had and probably never would, we had riches beyond his. We had friends that loved us and would do anything for us. I watched in the years to come how people of affluence began to leave him and even turn on him. His friendships were centered on money and success, not charity and love. Even though we were far younger than he was, the experience we had with our baby's death gave us years of wisdom beyond his. This was another example of the promise, "This will be a blessing in your life . . . if you will let it."

> *My son, peace be unto thy soul; thine adversity and thine afflictions shall be but a small moment; and then, if thou endure it well, God shall exalt thee on high; thou shalt triumph over all thy foes.*
>
> DOCTRINE & COVENANTS 121:7-8

My Heart Began to Pound

*O*ur youngest son, Kyle, was already a very mature three-and-a-half year-old before going through the experience of Brant's death. Because he thought of himself as an adult, he wanted to do things he wasn't capable of doing yet and he had to be told "no" quite often. All three-year-olds are this way to a point, but Kyle was beyond the, "to a point" line. He was intelligent beyond his years as well, and this only added to

> *We all contend with serious mortal frailties and hazards. Sickness, aging, and death are inescapable. Hardships and heartaches are a part of life's journey. For all these reasons and more, we need Heavenly Father's help.*
> — KEITH B. MCMULLIN —

his determination. Unfortunately, he still had the body and abilities of a three-and-a-half -year-old .

Not long after Brant's death, Kyle was determined to help me pin a pattern on some material. I said no, he persisted. I said no. He continued in his insistence of what he wanted to do, and I lost my temper. I reprimanded him and told him to go to his room and lay down. He left crying, and I continued with the task I was involved in.

As I finished, I realized it was really quiet and had been for some time. I began calling for Kyle. He always responded when I called for him and usually was always by my side. I began walking from room to room calling for him. I still didn't receive a response, and my heart began to pound.

Sometimes people, in their effort to comfort us, shared stories that planted the wrong seeds in our heads. Such was the case here. I kept hearing stories of people whose "tragedies" were "harder" than mine because they hadn't lost just one son but two. I began to believe brothers were often taken in pairs.

> *We know we are successful if we live so that we qualify for, receive, and know how to follow the Spirit.*
> — JULIE B. BECK —

As my steps quickened, my imagination began to run wild. I had looked in every room upstairs, where I expected him to be. Finally, I came to the room which had the back door that led to the backyard and the pool. I was crying by the time I opened the door. It was winter and cold outside. I hadn't been out to the pool or backyard since before Brant's death. I stood at the door for a moment and just looked. I knew I had to go check the pool. My heart was in my throat. I couldn't even swallow.

Slowly, I stepped down the cement step towards the pool. I inched my way on tip toes to the pool. I was so afraid of what I might find. As I got near the pool, I started to lean forward to look into the water, not wanting to get to close. I could see a clump at the bottom of the deep end where I was. I started to plead out loud, "No, no, please no." I stared into the bottom of the pool to try to make out what it was. My eyes finally focused through my tears, and I could see it was a towel. It had apparently blown into the pool, and nobody had bothered to retrieve it. I stood studying it for a moment. At a glance, it looked similar to the clump of a body. As I stood there, I realized how paranoid I was becoming.

My hands were shaking as I opened the back door and went inside the house. I had to find Kyle. Was it possible he had obeyed me and gone to his room and laid down? I finally went to the place I should have checked first. There was Kyle, downstairs in his bedroom, lying on his bed, peacefully and soundly asleep. I picked him up and held him and cried. *I will never get mad at him again.* I was so grateful to have him safe in my arms.

Unfortunately, it was foolish of me to think I would never get mad at him again. He was a little boy who had a very headstrong personality. He quite often wanted to do some of the most unbelievable things— and very often did. He still needed lots of guidance in his young life. The most foolish thing, however, is to let your emotions take over your ability to listen to the spirit. It took me years to get over the fear that I might lose Kyle, all because of fears I let enter in, due to stories others had shared with me. If I had taken the time to really ponder it, I would have realized I needed to set fear aside so I could receive true answers and feel peace.

Whatever hour God has blessed you with, take it with grateful hand, nor postpone your joys from year to year, so that in whatever place you have been, you may say that you have lived happily.

— HORACE —

He Was Talking Directly to Kyle

Just after Brant's death, the stores started getting their Christmas toys in. I shopped in the Mervyn's near us a lot; the same Mervyn's my sister had been to the day of Brant's drowning. One day, as we were in the store, more wandering than shopping, they had a Teddy Ruxpin on display. Our older children were in school, and we only had Kyle with us. We walked into the toy department and there he was, Teddy Ruxpin!

> *As disciples of the Lord Jesus Christ, we have enormous spiritual reservoirs of light and truth available to us . . . in our days of difficulty; we choose the road of faith.*
> — NEIL L. ANDERSEN —

He was so life like; it was as if he was talking directly to Kyle. His mouth was moving, and his eyes were opening and closing. I've never seen a reaction like Kyle had to that toy. To Kyle, it was a friend, a friend to take the place of the one he lost—his little brother. It was very expensive at that time, especially for the budget we were on.

As Christmas drew near, the Teddy Ruxpin was flying off the store shelves. It was turning into one of those toys that you would be lucky to get. We knew we had to splurge and buy it for Kyle. Somehow, we managed to fit it into our tight budget. It was far more than we would spend on our other children, but we knew they wouldn't care. They knew we bought it for him. We didn't usually tell them what anyone was getting, but that year we showed the other children what we were giving Kyle. They were all more excited for Christmas that year, for that reason alone, than I had ever seen them. They couldn't wait for Christmas morning; they all wanted to have the best spot to see Kyle's face.

As Kyle opened the Teddy Ruxpin and realized what it was, he started to cry. He was so happy. To watch his joy was overwhelming as he held that bear in his arms. We all sat on the floor around him and cried. It was as if Brant's spirit had touched the bear and given it a special light. It was one of the moments in life you hold onto. The closeness of our four children, holding onto one another for comfort and life, was indeed a unique moment.

*For the natural
man is an enemy to God,
and has been from the fall of Adam,
and will be, forever and ever, unless he
yields to the enticing of the Holy Spirit, and
putteth off the natural man and becometh a
saint through the atonement of Christ the Lord,
and becometh as a child, submissive, meek,
humble, patient, full of love, willing to submit
to all things which the Lord seeth fit
to inflict upon him, even as a child
doth submit to his father.*

— Mosiah 3:19 —

Are These Old Tears?

As I have already mentioned, I was three months pregnant at the time of Brant's death. On April first, five and a half months later, I gave birth to a beautiful little girl. She was our second daughter and the first girl after four boys in a row. I didn't have an ultrasound so I didn't know beforehand whether I was having a boy or a girl. I had been so fearful, especially in the couple of months before her birth, that I would have a boy. I truly feared this, not because I didn't cherish my boys and wouldn't feel the same for another son; it was the fear of the feeling I would be replacing Brant. I feared I wouldn't love a baby boy the same. I worried I would always feel he had taken Brant's place. Silly maybe, but in my mind it seemed a very real concern, at the time.

> Sometimes the messages (of angels) are more private. Occasionally the purpose is to warn. But most often it is to comfort, to provide some form of merciful attention, guidance in difficult times.
> — JEFFREY R. HOLLAND —

When Angela was born, and our doctor, the same doctor who spoke at Brant's graveside, announced she was a girl, I thought he was playing a cruel April fool's joke. After ten years of "It's a boy," it just didn't seem possible to have a girl. I looked at him without a reaction. Finally, he

The Spirit of God like a fire is burning!
The later day glory begins to come forth;
The visions and blessings of old are returning,
and angels are comingto visit the earth.

The Lord is extending the Saints' understanding,
restoring their judges and all as at first.
The knowledge and power of God are expanding;
the veil o'er the earth is beginning to burst.

We'll call in our solemn assemblies in spirit,
to spread forth the kingdom of heaven abroad,
That we through our faith may begin to inherit
he visions and blessings and glories of God.

How blessed the day when the Lamb and the lion
shall lie down together without any ire,
And Ephraim be crowned with his blessing in Zion,
and Jesus descends with His chariot of fire!

We'll sing and we'll shout with the armies of heaven,
hosanna, hosanna to God and the Lamb!
Let glory to them in the highest be given,
hence forth and forever, amen and amen.

— William W. Phelps

said, "Don't you want to see her?"

I thought, *Fine, here it goes, April fool's.* Lyle helped me up slightly so I could see and our doctor held her up. Sure enough, she really was a girl.

My doctor, as quickly as it was possible, began to cut the cord so he could place her in my arms. I was already crying, and he could see I needed to hold her. He handed my baby girl to the nurse and asked her to "wrap the baby and give her to her mother."

As she was wrapping her, the nurse said, "But I need to clean her first."

Our doctor emphatically replied, "This mother needs to hold her baby NOW!" At that, the nurse immediately placed her in my arms.

My crying turned to sobs as I held my precious daughter. Although she was still covered with the waxy film from birth, I kissed and kissed her all over her head. It didn't matter to me that she wasn't clean yet. My sobs intensified, and my doctor became concerned, "Are you in pain or are these old tears?" he asked. Through my sobs, I assured him they were old tears. He nodded lovingly because he already knew the answer I would give.

Lyle was standing at my side, and as he looked at our baby girl, he said with a very thoughtful attitude, "We can't name her Lacey." (Lacey was the name we had previously decided upon.)

I told him I didn't care what we named her; I was just happy to have her. He walked away and sat down on the couch nearby. This was very much out of character for him because he loved being right in the middle of the births of our children.

After about five minutes, he walked back over and said, "Angela. Her name needs to be Angela." I didn't question the name; she looked like an angel to me.

It wasn't long before we knew why he was prompted and inspired to name her Angela. She began talking at a very young age. Considering she was our sixth baby, we were pretty educated on the learning curve of a child, and Angela was very advanced. She was tiny in size and talking in full sentences by the time she was a year-and-a-half-old. Quite often, it shocked people who didn't know her and happened to hear her speak.

That's when we began to understand the reason for the special name. When we are asked by our Heavenly Father to sacrifice, we are always given gifts and blessings equal to that sacrifice, which in turn offers us comfort and peace. Such was the case with our little

Be not forgetful to entertain strangers: for thereby some have entertained angels unawares.
— HEBREWS 13:2 —

girl. I believe there is a veil placed upon us that keeps us from seeing our pre-earth and after death lives. In Angela's case, the veil was lifted, and she was given the gift of seeing those on the other side of the veil for a time. Eventually, the veil was dropped and she no longer had that gift, nor did she remember. But we remembered, and it was an unexpected comfort for the entire family.

The first time it occurred was when she was about fifteen months old. We were all in the master bedroom, where we often gathered together for closeness. We had about five thousand square feet in our home and spent most of our time in one room—our bedroom. There wasn't anything unusual about that evening, when out of nowhere, Angela said, "Brant's here." We all looked at her in shock. We hadn't even been talking about Brant.

"What did you say?" I asked.

She very calmly repeated herself, "Brant's here."

I believe my husband and I both asked at the same time, "Where? Where is he?"

She pointed to the corner of our room and said, "Over there." There was not a bit of emotion in her voice. She was very calm and matter-of-fact about her comment, as if it were common place and nothing to get too excited about.

We all stood up and walked to the center of the room. She then said, "He's going."

We asked, "Where is he going?" She walked out of our room, down the hall, through the front entry and out the front door. We all followed closely behind her. She walked out on the front porch and stood there looking up. We asked, "Where, Angela? Where is he?"

She pointed up towards the night sky. She then slightly shrugged her shoulders and said, "He's gone." We all stood there, just looking up at the stars. There was a feeling I can't describe.

After we stood there for a few minutes, we asked her again, "Can you see him?"

She again answered in an "oh well" attitude, "No, he's gone." She turned and went back into the house. We all looked at one another and filed back to our room to discuss the event.

This happened on several more occasions, until she was about two-and-a-half-years-old, and then it stopped. Although we prodded her now and then, asking if she had seen him, she would seem uninterested, as if she wasn't sure what we were talking about. Even though the experiences stopped, the gift Angela gave us was never forgotten.

For He shall give His angels charge over thee, to keep thee in all thy ways.

— PSALMS 91:11 —

I Pulled Brant Out of the Water

Not long after Brant died, we were really struggling with Kyle. He was having several concerning reactions. He refused to eat; he became anorexic. We begged him to eat any little bite. Within a year of Brant's death, he weighed less than Brant had at his death. There were a couple of foods he decided he liked. One was the "Hot Dog on a Stick," which they had at the mall, and the other was an "Egg McMuffin" from McDonald's. If he mentioned one or the other sounded good, we would get in the car and take him there to eat. Usually, he would eat one bite and maybe, if we were lucky, we could talk him into two or three bites, but that would be it.

> In this world abounding with misery, we are truly thankful for God's "great plan of happiness." His plan declares that men and women are "that they might have joy." That joy comes when we choose to live in harmony with God's eternal plan.
>
> — Russell M. Nelson —

He also liked watching "The Price Is Right" in the morning with me. It was just Kyle and I, and he loved that. I liked a snack of cottage cheese and Ritz crackers during the program. Because it was "our thing," Kyle thought that was okay and would eat a few crackers with cottage cheese on it. This one particular habit is probably what saved him, and maybe even me at the time. After working with him every day for about three years, we finally pulled him out of it. It formed some very interesting and special bonds centered on eating, that to this day are endearments.

The other concern was he fabricated stories. Some of these stories were so well done we really weren't sure at the time if they were true or not. Eventually, he would tell us they weren't true, which was how we discovered he was making up stories all the time. He grew out of this as well.

> *No other success can compensate for failure in the home.*
> — DAVID O. MCKAY —

The first story started at Brant's graveside ceremony, and it was the last story we finally found to be untrue. We began to question this story actually happening when we learned the others weren't true. He told his grandmother as they went to get the balloon that he had found Brant and tried to pull him out of the water. Lyle's mother came to us later, concerned that this could cause psychological problems, and suggested we might want to have someone talk to him. When we talked to him, he was very unconcerned and said he hadn't found Brant. Later, he told us again that he had found Brant, and he stuck to that story for a long time.

We had our bishop talk to him about a year after Brant's death, as we began to realize he was really good at making up stories. I mean these stories were very believable. They were also quite entertaining. Our bishop reported he felt Kyle was fine and we just needed to make sure we talked to him a lot. Kyle continued to maintain he had found Brant.

One day as the subject was again brought up, though we tried not to talk about it too much, Angela was standing there. She was about eighteen to twenty months old at the time. I happened to ask Kyle again if he had tried to pull Brant out of the water. He insisted he had. This didn't make sense to me because he wasn't wet when he came to me a few minutes later to tell me he couldn't find Brant. He was also very calm, and I knew he would have been more alarmed had he really found Brant. However, at this point, we were just trying to get him to tell us the truth.

Angela turned to me and said, "I pulled Brant out of the water."

I looked at her and said, "What?" I thought I had not heard her correctly.

She repeated, "I pulled Brant out of the water. I reached my arms down and pulled him up out of the water."

Remember, I was three months pregnant with her at the time of his death. I don't think anyone can be sure when the spirit enters the body of an unborn child. I believe that the spirit is near the body from the moment it is conceived. So I feel Angela's spirit was there when Brant drowned. I have become even more determined of this belief and conclusion because of the things Angela continued to insist on. She was just a baby herself and yet she understood what I was saying to Kyle. She repeated this to us again and again. About the time she quit seeing Brant, she also quit talking about pulling Brant out of the water.

When Angela was about five years old, I was telling someone about this special experience, and I asked her to tell them the story. It was the first time in a couple of years since we had said very much about it. She seemed confused so I told the story. When she was a little older, I asked her again about it, and she admitted she didn't have any idea what I was talking about. She said she didn't have any memory of it at all and still doesn't. I believe what really happened is that Angela's spirit was allowed the privilege of pulling Brant's spirit out of his body. That's why in her limited vocabulary, at her very young age, she explained it the way she did.

You, our youth of
today, are among the most
illustrious spirits to be born into
mortality in any age of the world . . .
be prepared to become leaders in
that glorious millennial day when
Christ himself will reign as King
of Kings and Lord of Lords.

— HAROLD B. LEE —

The Unexpected Happened

*W*hen Angela was three months old and it had been nine months since Brant's death, the very unexpected happened . . . I found out I was pregnant with my seventh child. It wasn't something we'd planned, but we were still very happy about it. We had always said we wanted five or six children, and this was just a bonus. Unfortunately, it meant months of being in bed sick. I was even worse this time because of the nearness of my last pregnancy.

It (increased spiritual strength) is like building muscle strength. You must break down your muscles to build them up. You push muscles to the point of exhaustion. Then they repair themselves, and they develop greater strength. Increased spiritual strength is a gift from God which He can give when we push in His service to our limits. Through the power of the Atonement of Jesus Christ, our natures can be changed.
— Henry B. Eyring —

The pain of Brant's death was still so deep, and that didn't help either. As my children and husband left in the morning, they would lay Angela by my side, and with Kyle's help, we handled it. Lyle tried to be there as much as he could, but he was trying to make sure we survived financially.

I finally made my first visit to the doctor when I was about six months along in my pregnancy. It is really not a very good idea to wait so long to see a doctor. I waited that long with Angela, too, but that was only because of Brant's death. Luckily, it worked out okay. This time I pushed my luck too far. I was still struggling with the emotional roller coaster I was on and, after six children, I was tired of sitting in the waiting room of a doctors' office. I guess any excuse will do when you're depressed

By the time I was about six and a half months into the pregnancy, I was having terrible stomach pains. I was traveling to our hometown for the doctor, so I could have our baby there. That is what I had done with all of our babies, from the time we'd moved away. My mother took me up to see my doctor in the hope of finding out what was causing the pain. Not only was I having severe stomach pain, but the Braxton-Hicks contractions seemed too strong for how far along I was.

> *Be thou an example of the believers, in word, in conversation, in charity, in spirit, in faith, in purity.*
> — I TIMOTHY 4:12 —

In examining me, my doctor found two concerning situations. I had a stomach ulcer, which wasn't a big surprise. The surprise was it wasn't more severe; but because of my pregnancy, the pain was almost unbearable at times. The second issue was I was already dilated to a three. That was a big problem; the last thing we needed was a premature, and possibly, a very sick baby.

My doctor's instructions were clear and very firm: I was to stay in bed at all times. I wasn't to get up for anything. He put me on medication for the ulcer, which worked like a miracle. I was so very grateful to have the excruciating pain in my abdomen gone. He also put me on a medication to stop the contractions. That wasn't so wonderful. I was glad to have the contractions stop, but the medication caused my heart to palpitate. So after being out of bed for one month, finally over the morning, noon and night sickness, I was back in bed to stay for the rest of my pregnancy.

There are always good things that come out of challenges such as this. I spent all of my time with my then nine-month-old baby and my other children when they were home. Our church asked for volunteers to come over several times a week to help clean our home. They also brought meals in all the time. The time I was able to spend with my children was precious. I will always remember the gift these sweet women gave me, allowing me to stay in bed for the sake of our new baby, and the bonus was the time I spent with our other children.

We were sure this time we would have a boy. We knew it just couldn't happen that we would have two girls in a row. We picked out the name, Thomas, as it was a family name in my husband's family. A couple of days before our baby was born; we decided we should have a girl's name as well. We decided on the same name. She would be called Tomi Jo if we had a girl. To our very unexpected and excited surprise, we did have a girl. We were especially thrilled because it meant our two babies, who were four days less than a year apart, were both girls. We knew they wouldn't be just sisters; they would be best friends, being so close in age. Tomi Jo was delivered within ten minutes of our arrival at the hospital and only two weeks early. She was one of the most precious, sweet babies. She hardly ever cried.

Our realization of what is most important in life goes hand in hand with gratitude for our blessings.
— THOMAS S. MONSON —

Prior to Brant's death and while I was expecting Angela, I felt strongly I was having twins. I had not been to the doctor before Brant died, and after his death, I felt one of the babies within me died. That was further confirmed when I passed a clot soon after Brant's death. Tomi Jo's surprise arrival, less than one year after Angela was born, made me feel she was Angela's lost twin.

A couple of years after the birth of Tomi Jo, we were looking through the meanings of the names of our children while at Disneyland. To my utter shock, we found the meaning of the name Tomi was "the twin." Sometimes we get messages and confirmations in the most amazing ways. I didn't need it confirmed by a doctor that I was having twins because I had it confirmed in so many other ways. The Spirit will carry a confirmation even as to what a child should be named. This is a good case in point of why we listen to the guidance of the Holy Spirit in every little aspect of our lives. Both Angela and Tomi were named by the Spirit, not by us.

To this day, they are as close as twin sisters could possibly be. Their weddings were nine months apart; their first babies were born nine months apart—both boys—and their second babies were born a week apart. They rarely live far from each other; at this time, they live only a block away from one another. I believe they were bonded in heaven and determined to be with one another on earth. If Tomi couldn't be born the same day, she made sure she was right behind.

TOMI

Derived from Thomas — Greek form of the Aramaic name "Te'oma" which meant "twin."

I learned several years later why it was so important for Tomi to come to us so soon after Angela. Sometimes the little hardships we endure just don't matter if it brings about an important purpose. Such was the case with Tomi Jo. It was somewhat of a hardship to bring her into the world so soon after Brant's death and Angela's birth, but a few years later she saved my life. I don't mean literally, but symbolically.

I was still fighting depression and sadness when Tomi was about four. She became my little shadow. She was the opposite of Angela in almost every way. Angela was a talker; Tomi Jo hardly spoke. She was a quiet giant, although not in stature. (She is now grown and a whopping five feet one inch tall.) A giant in spirit, however, she

The Lord is my light; then why should I fear?
By day and by night His presence in near.
He is my salvation from sorrow and sin;
this blessed assurance the Spirit doth bring.

The Lord is my light; tho clouds may arise,
faith, stronger than sight, looks up thru the skies.
Where Jesus forever in glory doth reign
then how can I ever in darkness remain?

The Lord is my light; the Lord is my strength.
I know in His might I'll conquer at length.
My weakness in mercy he covers with pw'r,
and, walking by faith, I am blest ev'ry hour.

The Lord is my light, my all and in all.
There is in His sight no darkness at all.
He is my Redeemer, my Savior, and King.
With Saints and with Angels His praises I'll sing.

The Lord is my light; He is my joy and my song.
By day and by night He leads, He leads me along.

— JAMES NICHOLSON

is and was, even at the age of four. As I said, she followed me everywhere, watching me, making sure I wasn't crying, as I very often did. I would actually try and be alone somewhere so I could cry. It was a difficult place to be, but it's where I was in my pain and recovery process.

One day I tried to sneak into the laundry room, very much planning to do laundry, but also feeling like I just wanted to sit down and cry. As I turned around, there stood Tomi Jo. I will never forget the look on her face; it's burned into my memory. There was a sadness and pleading in her eyes—a look that said, "Please, Mom, please be happy!" My poor little girl, she had never really had a happy mom. I went to her and kneeled down and just held her. I then got up and went straight into my bedroom and fell to my knees at the end of my bed and prayed. I don't know how long I prayed, but I know my prayer was heard.

I pleaded for help and guidance to lift me up and out of the state I was in. I felt an impression to get up and go into the living room, where there was a bookshelf full of books. I didn't know what books were on the shelves because they belonged to my husband's parents. We had moved back to our hometown about two months prior and were living in their home while they were away house sitting. I felt impressed to look at the books and just study their titles. Back and forth, up and down, I looked at the books in the shelves. I had no idea why or what I was looking for; I just felt something pull me up and lead me to the bookshelf.

Suddenly, a little white book seemed to stand out. I remember clearly the cover of the book because it was so simple yet heavenly. It was white with the titled embossed in gold. It was smaller than the standard size of a book and it was only about sixty or seventy pages long. It was a book on faith. It had been written by a woman, someone I had never heard of. She shared her own personal story and understanding of faith, the importance of faith and the need for us to learn of and gain faith in our lives. I don't recall anything especially profound that was said, but I remember that "aha" moment I felt as I read; that moment when I realized that I was lacking the faith I needed in my life to trust in the Lord with all of my heart, not just a little part of it. That prayer and book changed the direction of my life that day. Thanks to my little shadow, I found my life again. I found my love for life again—my love for my sweet children, my love for my dear husband—and I have never looked back. Thank you, Tomi.

Get Up and Win the Race

Whenever I start to hang my head in front of failure's face,
  my downward fall is broken by the memory of a race.
A children's race, young boys, young men; how I remember well,
  excitement sure, but also fear, it wasn't hard to tell.
They all lined up so full of hope, each thought to win that race
  or tie for first, or if not that, at least take second place.
Their parents watched from off the side, each cheering for their son,
  and each boy hoped to show his folks that he would be the one.
The whistle blew and off they flew, like chariots of fire,
  to win, to be the hero there, was each young boy's desire.
One boy in particular, whose dad was in the crowd,
  was running in the lead and thought, "My dad will be so proud."
But as he speeded down the field and crossed a shallow dip,
  the little boy who thought he'd win, lost his step and slipped.
Trying hard to catch himself, his arms flew everyplace,
  and midst the laughter of the crowd he fell flat on his face.
As he fell, his hope fell too; he couldn't win it now.
  Humiliated, he just wished to disappear somehow.
But as he fell his dad stood up and showed his anxious face,
  which to the boy so clearly said, "Get up and win that race!"
He quickly rose, no damage done, behind a bit that's all,
  and ran with all his mind and might to make up for his fall.
So anxious to restore himself, to catch up and to win,
  his mind went faster than his legs. He slipped and fell again.
He wished that he had quit before with only one disgrace.
  "I'm hopeless as a runner now, I shouldn't try to race.
But through the laughing crowd he searched and found his father's face
  with a steady look that said again, "Get up and win that race!"
So he jumped up to try again, ten yards behind the last.
  "If I'm to gain those yards," he thought, "I've got to run real fast!"

Exceeding everything he had, he regained eight, then ten...
  but trying hard to catch the lead, he slipped and fell again.
Defeat! He lay there silently. A tear dropped from his eye.
  "There's no sense running anymore! Three strikes I'm out! Why try?
I've lost, so what's the use?" he thought. "I'll live with my disgrace."
  But then he thought about his dad, who soon he'd have to face.
"Get up," an echo sounded low, "you haven't lost at all,
  for all you have to do to win is rise each time you fall.
Get up!" the echo urged him on, "Get up and take your place!
  You were not meant for failure here! Get up and win that race!"
So, up he rose to run once more, refusing to forfeit,
  and he resolved that win or lose, at least he wouldn't quit.
So far behind the others now, the most he'd ever been,
  still he gave it all he had and ran like he could win.
Three times he'd fallen stumbling, three times he rose again.
  Too far behind to hope to win, he still ran to the end.
They cheered another boy who crossed the line and won first place,
  head high and proud and happy—no falling, no disgrace.
But, when the fallen youngster crossed the line, in last place,
  the crowd gave him a greater cheer for finishing the race.
And even though he came in last with head bowed low, unproud,
  you would have thought he'd won the race, to listen to the crowd.
And to his dad he sadly said, "I didn't do so well."
  "To me, you won," his father said. "You rose each time you fell."
And now when things seem dark and bleak and difficult to face,
  the memory of that little boy helps me in my own race.
For all of life is like that race, with ups and downs and all.
  And all you have to do to win is rise each time you fall.
And when depression and despair shout loudly in my face,
  another voice within me says, "Get up and win that race!"

— Attributed to Dr. D.H. "Dee" Groberg

My Heart Went Out to Her

Several months after Brant's death, we reread some of the cards and letters we had set aside as "special." One in particular was from a woman in our church. We weren't well acquainted at all with her. She wrote us of the loss of her own son, and it sounded, from her letter as if it had been recent. She told us she would really like to visit with us and gave us her phone number

> *Never let a problem to be solved become more important than a person to be loved.*
> — THOMAS S. MONSON —

as well as her place of work. We decided to go to her workplace, as it was a church bookstore, and we felt it would be a good place to meet her. We didn't want to talk long and thought it would force the conversation to be short. However, we did feel compelled to talk to her.

When we arrived it was quiet, and very few people were there. We asked for her, not even sure what she looked like. She was older than we had expected her to be. I could tell she was very surprised to see us, as though she really never expected us to respond to her invitation. I'm not sure she knew who we were at first either by her reaction. We almost needed to remind her of who we were, but she still seemed very happy we had come.

Yesterday I met a stranger . . .
today this stranger is my friend.
Had I not taken the time to say hello,
or return a smile, or shake a hand,
or listen, I would not have known
this person. Yesterday would have
turned into today, and our chance
meeting would be gone.
Yesterday I hugged someone very
dear to me. Today they are gone . . .
and tomorrow will not bring them back.
Wouldn't it be nice if we all knew
tomorrow they would be here?
But this is not to be, so take the time
today to give a hug, a smile,
and "I love you."

— AUTHOR UNKNOWN —

She began to talk about her own situation and her son when he died. He had also drowned. The circumstance surrounding her son's death was more than strange. She said she had felt she would lose him early, so she more than protected and guarded him from ever getting far from her sight. One day when he was about two years of age, he managed to get out of their very secure backyard and drowned in a culvert which had hardly any water in it.

As she told us her story, she wept. My heart went out to her for her pain. I then asked her how long it had been since he died. Her response was, "It has been twenty years."

I was taken aback but tried not to show my surprise. As we walked away, after embracing one another, I felt such closeness with her. It was then Lyle and I realized the pain never goes completely away. We realized we would never quit missing Brant. He would always be a part of our life, and we would never quit loving him the way we did now.

*Sometimes the
very moments that
seem to overcome us with
suffering are those that
will ultimately suffer
us to overcome.*

— JOSEPH B. WIRTHLIN —

Guardian Angel

*N*ot quite a year after Brant died, early one morning, Darci came into our room very excited, yet reverent at the same time. She wanted to hear the song. "What song?" I asked.

"The song Dad was writing last night," she anxiously responded. I knew Lyle was up really late into the night, and I could feel a very special spirit around him, but I didn't know, nor had I asked what he was doing.

The word angel is used in various ways. A person who is a divine messenger is called an Angel.

See: Angel (Bible Dictionary)

Darci went on to explain. Something had awakened her in the middle of the night. She didn't know why, but she felt impressed to get up. She left her room and could see light coming from the family room so that's where she felt she should go. As she entered the family room, she saw her father on the couch. She explained, "There was a very special feeling about him. He had a soft, yet deeply intense look on his face." She felt he was receiving revelation for something and felt it was a song.

Lyle has always had a gift for writing songs. She told me she could feel Brant's spirit and thought the song would be about him. She interrupted her dad and asked him if he was writing a song. He told her

GUARDIAN ANGEL

Guardian Angel, sweet angel,
where did you get your name?
Come dream with me and I will explain.
With a mother and father into the
world I came, then not knowing
the rules to the game.
(Chorus)
For I am to be their Guardian Angel,
in times of trouble today and tomorrow,
Yes, I am to be their Guardian Angel
in heaven or earth, in joy and in sorrow.
The problem for now is how do I go away?
How do I tell them that I must not stay?
For we made a pact before I was born,
that I'd come to earth and leave them to mourn.
(Repeat 1ˢᵗ Chorus)
Now lest ye cry of this sad tale,
let me remind thee by heavenly mail;
that the thing we call death
is not to be the end,
but the start of forever and ever, my friend.
(Chorus)
For we should all be Guardian Angels,
in times of trouble today and tomorrow.
Yes, we should all be Guardian Angels,
in heaven or earth in joy and in sorrow.
Who's your Angel, sweet Angel?
Who is your love forever?
Whom do you cherish forever and ever?
With all the right vows and covenants,
it will be the same,
sealed up with love and in His Holy name.
(Chorus)
Yes, we should all be Guardian Angels
one to another, brother to brother.
We should all be Guardian Angels,
one to another brother to brother.

— LYLE G. WOOD

he was. She felt she should not interrupt any further, him or the Spirit that was around him, so she went back to bed.

Needless to say, she was anxious and excited to hear the song the next morning. She felt it would be something she would sing and hopefully someday record. That was her dream, to be a singer.

At this point I was excited and curious as well, so even though my husband had not slept much, we woke him and asked him about the song. He motioned to where it was laying. Darci picked it up and read the words, the inspired words of Brant's mission. It brought tears to our eyes then and still does to this day. Lyle said he was still working on the melody but had a pretty good feeling for it as well.

He was awake now since he couldn't sleep through the commotion we were creating and proceeded to sing the song with the words. I felt it was truly inspired. I know songs like this come after the trial of your faith. They come as a comfort from the Holy Spirit. Lyle said as he went to bed the night before, he couldn't sleep. The words started to fill his mind, and he had to get up and write them down. He was in the middle of this spiritual experience when Darci came in. The Spirit was strong, and he was listening, receiving and writing. This was not his song; he was simply an instrument in the hands of the Lord. He called the song "Guardian Angel."

God does notice us, and He watches over us. But it is usually through another person that He meets our needs. Therefore, it is vital that we serve each other.
— SPENCER W. KIMBALL —

Dad Died

Two years after Brant's death, Angela was seventeen months and Tomi was five months of age, my father had begun to have chest pains. He had already had a heart attack about five years prior, and we knew it was serious. He was only fifty-eight years old, but we had a family history of heart problems. The doctors decided he needed a triple by-pass and scheduled the surgery. There

> We will never regret the kind words spoken or the affection shown. Rather, our regrets will come if such things are omitted from our relationships with those who mean the most to us.
> — Thomas S. Monson —

were complications during the surgery that they didn't discover until later. As they tried to take him off the ventilator, he could no longer breathe on his own. They discovered that during surgery his diaphragm had been damaged, and he couldn't then, nor would he ever be able to breathe, without the help of a ventilator.

We visited him every day, which was difficult because of our young family, but also because he was in the same hospital where Brant had died. The day the doctor told my sister and me that he didn't think our father would live was like déjà vu. I didn't feel I could stand it.

I became hysterical and said to the doctor, "But you said this was like having a tonsillectomy." He didn't know what to say. He just looked at my sister, who is a nurse, in desperation. As she put her arms around me in comfort, I heard her quietly explain to the doctor why my reaction was so extreme. I was having, so to speak, a double whammy. My father lived for fifteen days in the hospital and was unconscious after the first two days.

The night before my father died, Lyle felt prompted to go visit him. We were just leaving a Cub Scout pack meeting for Courtney and Matthew, and it was fairly late. I was tired and needed to get our babies to bed. He was so insistent that we needed to go to the hospital, which was more than a half hour drive away, so I finally agreed. We gave instructions to Darci about the children and left for the hospital. It was after 9 p.m. when we arrived, and they were bathing him so we stayed in the hall a moment. I could see he had regained consciousness and I was so excited.

As we entered his room, I could tell he was very alert and had a very different countenance about him. There was a beautiful feeling, both in the room and about my father. He smiled when he saw us, more with his eyes than anything else, as he was on the ventilator. I hugged him as tight as I could and told him I loved him. Lyle did the same.

We started to talk to him, but he was very distracted with something—or better yet, someone—over in the opposite corner from where we were standing next to him. I kept saying, "Dad," and he would look back at us for a moment or two, smiling with his eyes, showing through them he loved us, but then his head would slowly turn back again to the corner of the room. Lyle and I looked at one another after this had happened several times and said, "What is going on in that corner?" It didn't faze my father; he just kept intently watching the corner with the happiest, most peaceful look on his face. The look he had now was a far cry from the look he'd had two weeks ago, just before he went into the coma. That was a look of complete panic and fear.

In an effort to make a one-sided conversation, I started telling him that our kids had come to see him. I asked him if he remembered, but he didn't look at me. I continued with, "Dad, do you remember? We brought Darci, and she sang for you." My father had always been so proud of Darci's singing talent, especially at her young age. Nearly every time he saw her, he wanted her to sing. As I started telling him this, Lyle began unconsciously humming the song she sang, which was the song Lyle wrote about Brant. It is a beautiful song, and Lyle also has a beautiful voice. My father would always tease Lyle that he couldn't sit quiet for a moment; he always had to be humming, which is true.

As soon as Lyle started to hum, my father, for the first time since we arrived, turned his head with a jolt back towards us. Lyle took the cue and started quietly singing the song. My dad's face was remarkable to watch. There was such pure light and awareness in it. I could see he remembered the song, and he knew Darci sang it to him while he was in the coma. He didn't take his eyes off of Lyle the entire time he sang the song. But as soon as he finished, Dad's head turned back, and his eyes again went to the corner. We only stayed a few more minutes. I kissed my dad and said goodbye. He hardly noticed we'd left. It didn't bother us, though; we were left with such a sweet, peaceful feeling. If my dad could have spoken, I'm sure he would have rejoiced in speaking the words that are written in the side bars of these pages.

I've always wondered why my dad's attention stayed focused on us during the singing of the song. Was it because he remembered Darci singing it to him while he was in the coma? Or was it because he recognized it from our pre-earth life? All things are created spiritually before they are created physically so I submit this thought: the song "Guardian

I am a part of the fellowship of the unashamed. I have the Holy Spirit power. The die has been cast. I have stepped over the line. The decision has been made. I am a Disciple of Jesus Christ.

I won't look back, let up, slow down, back away, or be still. My past is redeemed, my present makes sense, and my future is secure. I am finished and done with low living, sight walking, small planning, smooth knees, colorless dreams, tame visions, mundane talking, chintzy giving, and dwarfed goals. I no longer need preeminence, prosperity, position, promotions, plaudits or popularity. I don't have to be right, first, tops, recognized, praised, regarded, or rewarded.

I now live by presence, learn by faith, love by patience, lift by prayer and labor by power. My pace is set, my gait is fast, my goal is heaven, my road is narrow, my way is tough, my companions few, my guide is reliable, my mission is clear. I cannot be bought, compromised, deterred, lured away, turned back, diluted, or delayed. I will not flinch in the face of sacrifice, hesitate in the presence of adversity, negotiate at the table of the enemy, ponder at the pool of popularity, or meander in the maze of mediocrity. I won't give up, back up. Let up. Or shut up until I've preached up, prayed up, paid up, stored up, and stayed up for the cause of Christ. I am a Disciple of Jesus Christ. I must go until He returns, give until I drop, preach until all know, and work until He comes. And when He comes to get His own, He will have no problem recognizing me. My colors will be clear for

"I am not ashamed of the Gospel, because it is the power of God for the Salvation of everyone who believes . . ."

(Romans 1:16)

— AUTHOR UNKNOWN

Angel" already existed.

As I've already mentioned, we were really struggling with Kyle and his habit of not eating. The next morning, Kyle decided he wanted an Egg Mcmuffin for breakfast. So, as we did quite often in an effort to get him to eat, we jumped in the car and went to McDonald's.

While we were gone, my father's condition worsened, and my sister continually tried to reach us. We had just arrived back home when the phone rang. My husband answered it, and then gave it to me with a strange look on his face. It was my sister; she was calling from the hospital. Her voice was strained and upset. "Where have you been?" she questioned.

"I've been calling and calling." I explained where we had been, and then she blurted out, "Dad died."

I had just been with him the night before, and he was so bright, so well. As we drove to the hospital, Lyle and I talked about our experience with my father the night before. We both realized who he had been so intrigued with, and he was apparently quite anxious to be with. We were both so grateful for those last moments with my father. It was more than special; it was a testimony to us of the other side of the veil. I know many families have similar experiences when loved ones leave, and I believe they are given to us for comfort so we will know we're not alone. Angels do walk and talk with us. I believe Brant was one of those angels with my father that night.

O that I were
an angel, and could
have the wish of mine heart,
that I might go forth and speak
with the trump of God, with
a voice to shake the earth,
and cry repentance unto
every people!

— ALMA 29:1 —

Angel Messenger

*A*nother angel with us, not one from the other side, was and is our daughter Angela. At the time of my father's death, Angela was seventeen months old. As I have mentioned, she was bright and could talk extremely well for her age. She was talking in full sentences very clearly. I believe she was given the "gift of tongues" for our comfort and learning. She was also one of those from this side who walked and talked with angels. This was further verified during my father's viewing.

We felt it was best to leave our children home as the viewing might have been too upsetting for them. When we arrived home, I went to the kitchen to clean up some messes. Lyle came in with Angela and said to her, "Tell Mommy what you told me."

> *Whenever you hear music an angel is speaking to you. Your guardian angel helps you find a place when you feel there's no place to go. Angels carry high-beam light to help you through the darkest hour. Angels know that love is the only four-letter-word. We are always "angels on call" for a friend. Angels are with you every step of the way and help you soar with amazing grace. After all, we are angels in training . . . all we have to do is spread our wings and fly!*
>
> — UNKNOWN —

Without thinking twice, Angela began to talk. "Grandpa was here. I kissed his face, but I kissed Brant more. Then they ran to Grandma." Lyle and I discussed what Angela may have meant by this experience. She was so young, and although she spoke very well and it made sense to her, we had to interpret what she was saying. We believe because Angela could still see those from the other side of the veil, my father, accompanied by Brant, came to visit her. She let us know who was there by saying, "I kissed Grandpa's face" and then expressed her special love and connection to Brant by saying, "but I kissed Brant more". We were thrown a little when she said, "They ran to Grandma" because my mother was still alive. We concluded this—because of her limited vocabulary she didn't know how to describe the quickness with which a spirit will move so she used the word "ran". By her saying, "They ran to Grandma," we assumed they communicated with her in some way and they intended to visit my mother next. This experience confirmed even further to us that Brant had been with my father the night we visited him in the hospital. It also confirmed to us the very existence of a life after death and that we are received by those we love, even family members.

Angela was too young to even conceive the idea of making up a story like that. Her attitude was, once again, very matter-of-fact, as if she didn't understand why we were getting so excited. This was all commonplace to her and her life at that time. She literally walked and talked with angels. Sadly, she can't remember her experiences. However, they really weren't for her. She didn't need them to know the truth of our purpose here; she still remembered being with our Heavenly Father. These experiences were for us, all of us. We don't remember our pre-earth life and sometimes forget why we are here. Angela's visits with Brant and my dad, and her gifts that allowed her to be capable of sharing them, were precious reminders for us. She doesn't need to remember because we will not forget.

Not long after all the amazing experiences we had with Angela, we looked up the meaning of her name in a baby book. The meaning of Angela is "angel messenger."

ANGELA

From the Medieval Latin name 'Angelus' which was derived from the name of the heavenly creature; (itself derived from the Greek word 'Angelos" meaning "messenger")

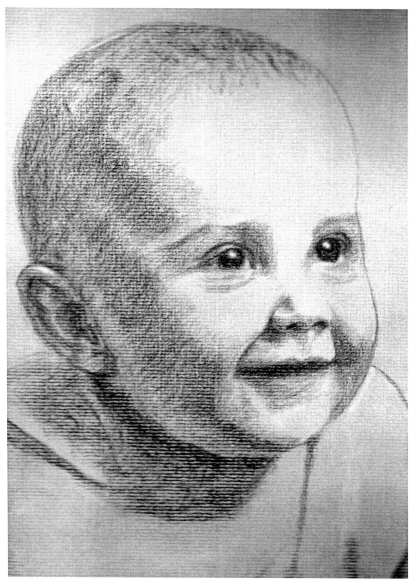

L. Brant Wood, age 6 months   Drawing by Lori Wood

Delayed Reaction to Brant's Death

Sometimes the effects of a trauma in your life won't manifest itself for years, and everyone reacts in different ways. With children, you have to be aware at all times. Even though something may not seem to be related at all, it may actually be an underlying force that starts the action. The experience we had with our eldest son and second child, Courtney exemplified that.

> *This is our one and only chance at mortal life—here and now. The longer we live, the greater is our realization that it is brief. Opportunities come, and then they are gone. I plead with you not to let those most important things pass you by . . .*
> — THOMAS S. MONSON —

It has taken years for me to recognize this, and that's why I share it—to help others realize that any out of the ordinary behavior should be dealt with, and not just brushed aside as a stage they might be going through.

Courtney, as with the other children, is very intelligent and did very well in school. The difference with Courtney was it seemed almost effortless for him to get high marks in school. Learning and applying what he learned came easily and naturally, and he enjoyed it. It was all second nature to him.

You are not just ordinary young men and young women. You are choice spirits, many of you having been held back in reserve for almost 6,000 years to come forth in this day, at this time when the temptations, responsibilities, and opportunities are the very greatest. . . .

— EZRA TAFT BENSON —

Two years after Brant's death, when he was in the fifth grade—a very important year—Courtney started to struggle with school. It wasn't that he didn't grasp what was being taught; it was his lack of desire to go to school, and his grades obviously reflected it. If you miss a lot of school, your grades can drop and Courtney was missing a lot of school due to an unusual illness. However, we ensured that he made up the work and understood all the concepts. We blamed his sickness on a gland problem he had, which was true to a point, but his sick days surpassed even what was normal for that. He simply did not want to go to school, and his glands, which were often swollen, became a convenient excuse for him.

Our children's school had a new principal, and nearly all the teachers who had previously taught there left to teach elsewhere. Consequently, almost every teacher was new and, in most cases, new to teaching. In the past, I had requested my children's teachers from year to year, knowing or finding out who the best teachers were. I did this to avoid ever having another situation with a teacher like we'd had with Matthew when he was in kindergarten. I would never again have anything but the best for them if possible. I believed my children, and all children, deserve the best in teachers; unfortunately, not all teachers are created equal.

Courtney's teacher that year was new. She seemed nice enough, but I decided to volunteer to help in the classroom one time just so I could observe. This was as much to try and understand why Courtney didn't want to go to school as any other reason. I was sadly disappointed in what I witnessed in the teacher. This, along with his sickness, was a good enough reason for his lack of incentive for school. We might have held our breath and just muddled through the year, but we felt we needed to do more.

We found that when Courtney went back to school after a period of sickness, he wasn't turning in the work he had done while at home. He went from being a straight "A" student to getting "C's" on his report card, and he just didn't care. Increasingly, he would come to me in the morning and say he was sick.

What I realize now, and should have realized at the time, was Courtney was having a delayed reaction to Brant's death, and he was depressed. He was usually a very happy, energetic boy, but even in his personality, he just wasn't the same. We decided we needed to take some kind of action.

If you don't change your direction, you may end up where you are headed.
— UNKNOWN —

Armed with what I saw in the classroom while I had observed, we decided to move him to another school. This was pretty drastic, but we felt we needed to do this for Courtney's sake. At this time, we were going more by the guidance from within rather than actually knowing what was wrong and what we should do. We went to the school district with our petition to change schools.

As the superintendent met with us and Courtney, he looked over Courtney's past school records and his records of that year and agreed with us. The school superintendent also voiced his concerns with the school because of the extreme changes that had taken place with their teachers that year. He gave us our choice of a couple of other schools that were proven to be academically advanced in the district. We decided on one and made an appointment with the principal.

We met with the principal on the appointed day, and we were very impressed. It was obvious why the school was so good after meeting with her. She did have some concerns she shared with us. First, the distance we would be driving Courtney every day, but more importantly the fact that we would be bringing Courtney into the school in the middle of the year. She knew her classes in fifth grade were further advanced than the other schools in the district, and Courtney would be coming from a situation where he was behind, both because of the school and his constant illness. She didn't try to push us off on another alternative however. She really wanted to come up with a solution that was best for Courtney. I could feel she cared about Courtney, and she was very impressed with him as a young man.

And as all have not faith, seek ye diligently and teach one another words of wisdom; yea, seek ye out of the best books words of wisdom; seek learning, even by study and also by faith . . . . Establish a house, even a house of prayer, a house of fasting, a house of faith, a house of learning.
— Doctrine & Covenants 88:118-119 —

She asked us if we had considered home school. We had never heard of it. The principal then proceeded to explain the rights we had as parents to teach our children in our home. She was very supportive of the home schooling program. She also shared with us the fact that there was a group of parents in the city which had created an association to help one another with teaching aids, ideas and books. The group was a very large and city-wide. The school district was also involved with home-taught children; they tested them at the end of each school year with the same tests they used within the public school system. She convinced us to try this method and said if it didn't work, Courtney would be more than welcome in her school.

We thought this sounded like a viable solution, and we agreed to try it.

Because I didn't know how much he may have missed, I decided to start Courtney at the beginning of the fifth grade books. He spent about three hours a day in his school work. That included all the subjects required by the school district, as well as accomplishing his assignments. I spent approximately an hour every day teaching him the concepts. We had the same books that were being used in the schools, along with a teacher's manual. Every subject was the same as taught in the school and yet Courtney was finished within three hours a day. We started about halfway through the school year, and he was finished with every book from beginning to end in every subject a little before the end of that school year. He was completely prepared for the end of the year testing which was held at the school district offices. Courtney received "A's" in nearly every subject. It was an amazing experience for me to home school him. Not only did I discover how very intelligent he is, but it opened up a special time and closeness with him.

> *And besides this, giving all diligence, add to your faith, virtue; and to virtue knowledge; and to knowledge temperance; and to temperance patience; and to patience godliness; and to godliness brotherly kindness; and to brotherly kindness charity.*
> — 2 Peter 1:5-7 —

This was impressive and important, but not as much as what we gained in other ways. The individual time I spent with Courtney let me understand and help him with his acceptance of his brother's death. Death can be a difficult thing for young people to comprehend and that needed to be dealt with. I usually handled this through the normal day to day chats we had. Because of this experience, we discovered a wonderful method of having special time with each of our children. We kept Courtney in home school the following year as well. By the time he went into the seventh grade, he was stable and prepared. His grades were always top, and he graduated from high school with several college credits as well. Not only did he have these accomplishments, he was also a very confident and happy person. To this day, he is successful in all he does.

I believe his fifth grade year was a pivotal point, and Courtney could have gone a different direction had he not established who he was by being at home. I feel he was insecure and possibly depressed because of the loss of his brother. By being at home, he became grounded through the love of his family and their constant companionship. He realized, subconsciously, he was not alone. Was it by accident or divine intervention (I prefer the second as the answer) that we discovered this way of spending special time with Courtney?

We continued this practice with every one of our children. We found the success of our children always stemmed from what was taught at home. Once again the echo, "This will be a blessing in your life if you will let it."

*I am so
grateful that I
am seeing the truth
of life with more
clarity every day.*

— UNKNOWN —

A Rare and Sacred Experience

One night when our children were all asleep and we had just gone to bed, we had a very rare and sacred experience. It completely confused us at first, but as time went by and we understood, we found it to be very, very special.

We had turned the lights out in our master bedroom but were both wide awake, not talking, just enjoying the quiet of the night you come to treasure with a large, noisy family. We heard a child say, "Mom." I looked toward the sound. Standing next to our dresser, at the foot of our bed was a boy about four years old. There was enough light coming through the window from outside that we could see him, but it was dark enough, and he stood far enough away, that we could not see who it was. At least we didn't recognize him clearly.

Our personal journey through life provides us with many special experiences that become building blocks of faith and testimony.
— RONALD A. RASBAND —

I responded with, "What?" He didn't say anything; he just stood very still looking at us. I said again, not knowing but thinking this must be Kyle, "Kyle, what do you want?" Silence was all there was. Again, I spoke. "Come here," I commanded. He remained still, not moving from where he stood. I wanted him to come to me so I could put my arms around him and find out what was troubling him. If it were Kyle, he would have been over to me after the first word spoken. This little guy, however, just stood there, not saying another word or moving even the slightest muscle.

At that point, I became frustrated that he wouldn't tell me what he wanted or come to me so I could look in his face. Not knowing what more I could say or do, I said, "Go back to bed." At that command, he was gone. I immediately looked toward our double bedroom doors, which were on the opposite side of our bedroom. They were still closed, as they had been when we'd gone to bed. I realized I had not heard them open when the boy appeared or close when he left. I looked around my room, but he was gone. I kept looking towards the dresser where he had been standing; I could see the corner of the dresser very clearly now. There was no mistake— someone had been standing there.

Please notice how the power of the Spirit carries the message unto but not necessarily into the heart . . . ultimately . . . the content of a message and the witness of the Holy Ghost penetrate into the heart only if a receiver allows them to enter.
— David A. Bednar —

He'd never said another word. All he said was the initial "Mom," which caused us both to look over at him. My husband didn't say anything during the five minutes or so this all happened, he just watched. I said, "That was strange."

He responded, "Yes, it was." We finally drifted to sleep.

We both awoke very early the next morning. Lyle said to me, "What was that all about last night?"

"I don't know. Was it Kyle?" I asked, even though I already knew it wasn't.

He immediately called for Darci who was getting ready for school across the hall. She came in, and he asked her to go get Kyle, which she did. She could tell there was a sense of urgency in her father's voice. Kyle came in very sleepy-eyed. We proceeded to ask him what he'd wanted last night when he came into our room. He said he had not come into our room last night. Mind you, Kyle was about six-and-a-half at this time and had a memory like an elephant. The likelihood of him coming in our room and being part of all that had happened, then not remembering, was, to say the least, impossible. However, we pressed him saying, "Yes, don't you remember? You stood right there and said, 'Mom.'" Again, he insisted he had not come into our bedroom the night before. We told him, "Okay, you can go back to bed."

Darci had been listening and asked what had happened. We told her the story. Her immediate response was, "Was it Brant?" I didn't know. I said it didn't look like Brant.

Lyle said, "It couldn't have been Brant. He was too big." I agreed and said I was sure it wasn't.

Darci asked how big he was, and we said, "Four-ish." She asked if he was smaller than Kyle, and we both nodded our heads. I said he was about a head shorter, and Lyle agreed.

> God allows us to be the guardians, or the gatekeepers, of our own hearts. We must, of our own free will, open our hearts to the Spirit, for He will not force Himself upon us.
> — GERALD N. LUND —

Then Darci asked, "What did he want?" We told her that we had no idea, but I think we all really knew. He came older than Brant so we would know he wasn't Brant. He came younger than Kyle so there wouldn't be any question in our minds—he wasn't Kyle. He called me "Mom" and then didn't say another word. He refused to move from his position at the end of our bed area. We both saw him and heard him, and then he vanished as quickly as he had appeared.

I refused at that time to admit I was supposed have another baby, let alone agree to have one. Tomi was only eighteen months and Angela was two-and-a-half. They were still babies, and I had my hands full. I couldn't even bear the thought of going through another pregnancy. I would get so sick, and after seven pregnancies, I knew that wasn't going to change. By the time I had Tomi, my body was in pain everywhere, and I didn't think I could even carry another baby. So whoever he was, I knew I couldn't have him. Consequently, I chose to ignore the experience.

Not long after this experience, I woke up from a dream in which I was changing a baby boy's diaper. It was so real and vivid. I had to lay there quite a while in that groggy, early morning confusion, trying to figure out whose diaper I had changed. I knew it was a dream, but it also seemed too real to be a dream. Suddenly, I felt that piercing in my heart, and I knew I was pregnant. I was so distraught. My husband, however, was thrilled. He knew we were supposed to have that little boy, and as far as he was concerned, "the more the merrier." I was so depressed, I just kept crying.

> We feel things in our hearts. In the scriptures, the prophets teach that personal revelation is closely linked to the heart. For example: Mormon taught, "Because of meekness and lowliness of heart cometh the visitation of the Holy Ghost." (Moroni 8:26) Alma said, "He that will harden his heart, the same receiveth the lesser portion of the word; and he that will not harden his heart, to him is given the greater portion of the word." (Alma 12:10) And the Psalmist simply wrote, "The Lord is nigh unto them that are of a broken heart." (Psalms 34:18)
>
> — GERALD N. LUND —

One day, when I was nearly five months along in my pregnancy, I was having an especially hard day. I just kept crying. Lyle, in desperation, finally called my mother and asked her to come over. He told her, "I just don't know what to do to make her feel better."

My mother lived on the other side of the city, about a half an hour drive from me. I wasn't aware Lyle had called her and so wasn't expecting her to walk in our door. As I walked down the hallway, she came around the corner. When I saw her, I again broke into tears. She put her arms around me as I sobbed and these are the words she said to me. "Lori, I promise you, this little boy will be one of the greatest blessings in your life." And then she held me tight. I immediately felt strength come into me. I believed what she promised me. I believe it was a matriarchal blessing the Lord allowed her to give me. I never cried again.

When our son Jordan was born, the placenta had an emblazoned, heart-shaped tattoo on it. It was dark maroon in color and covered the major part of the sac. Our doctor was about sixty-five years-old and an obstetrician. He had delivered thousands of babies. He said he had never seen anything like it. It was a perfect heart. I believe it was a sign given to us, a sign to let us know the love the Lord had for this little boy, the love Jordan would bring to our family, the love Heavenly Father had for us because we were willing to bring this last son into our family and maybe a message from Brant letting us know he loved us. We have always told Jordan he was *"born in a heart"*. He has lived up to the reputation given him the day he was born. He is all heart.

The condition of our hearts directly affects our sensitivity to the spiritual things. Let us make it a part of our everyday striving to open our hearts to the Spirit.

— GERALD N. LUND —

So Broken-Hearted

*J*t was couple of months after Brant's death that Lyle and I decided to go to a mall downtown. It was a very high end mall and one we rarely went to. On this particular day, we just wanted to get away from the "normal" and do something different. We both had an especially hard day with our grief over Brant and felt a change of environment would alter our focus.

The dial on the wheel of sorrow eventually points to each of us. At one time or another, everyone must experience sorrow. No one is exempt.

— JOSEPH B. WIRTHLIN —

We were browsing through one of the more expensive department stores when we ran into a friend. He was a year younger than I was in school, so we didn't know him very well. He had moved to the same city we were living in to work for my cousin in one of the very nice hotels in town. We knew him better because of his workplace than we had known him in high school. He was wandering with the same, seemingly aimless attitude as we. He had heard about our son's death and stopped to offer his condolences.

He immediately went on to ask if we knew about his divorce. We were both rather stunned but tried not to let it show. "No, we hadn't heard," we replied. We had been pretty secluded as far as knowing or hearing things of that nature. With hardly a moment's pause, he went on. He told us the story of his divorce and shared with us his broken-hearted feelings. He shared with us how he had not wanted the divorce to happen and didn't know how it had even come to that. He shared, without stopping, for twenty, maybe thirty, minutes. The only comments we made the entire time were how sorry we were over and over.

Because Jesus Christ suffered greatly, He understands our suffering. He understands our grief. We experience hard things so that we too may have increased compassion and understanding for others.
— Joseph B. Wirthlin

I think he must have suddenly realized how much he was almost babbling because he stopped suddenly and looked at us as if embarrassed. He then again acknowledged our son's death and how sorry he was, excused himself somewhat abruptly, and left. We watched him as he hurried to the elevators we were near and stepped in. We stood there for a moment, then started walking and talking about the experience.

We both realized what a blessing this encounter had been. Although our grief was great, this helped us realize we weren't alone in grief. There is grief brought on by all kinds of hardships in our lives. We are all given our own set of trials, and it's up to us to handle them the best we can, then pick ourselves up and go on. It's not an overnight recovery for anyone. We need to go through the proper steps of grieving. It's important to go through every step. Most people do this naturally, but some try to be heroes, or think they are bigger and stronger and intentionally skip through the steps of wellness. This is not good. Eventually, all steps must be covered or you don't heal; it doesn't matter what the cause of your grief might be.

These were the things we realized as we stood there listening to our friend. He was as heart-broken as we were. His pain was as deep as ours. As a matter of fact, we both commented that we would take our trial over his any day. That may sound strange, especially as commonplace as divorce has become, and the death of your child is so intense, but we still had each other. We

When upon life's billows you are tempest-tossed,
when you are discouraged, thinking all is lost,
count your many blessings; name them one by one,
and it will surprise you what the Lord has done.

Are you ever burdened with a load of care?
Does the cross seem heavy you are called to bear?
Count your many blessings; ev'ry doubt will fly,
and you will be singing as the days go by.

When you look at others with their lands and gold,
think that Christ has promised you His wealth untold.
Count you many blessings; money cannot buy
your reward in heaven nor your home on high.

So amid the conflict, whether great or small,
do not be discouraged; God is over all.
Count your many blessings; angels will attend,
help and comfort give you to your journey's end.

Count your blessings; name them one by one.
Count your blessings; see what God hath done.
Count your blessings; name them one by one.
Count your many blessings; see what God hath done.

— JOHNSON OATMAN JR. —

had each other to hold onto; we had each other to cry with; and we had and still have each other forever. My pain felt less overwhelming and out of control than our friend's seemed to be. We knew where our son was and that we would be with him again as long as we lived our lives according to our Heavenly Father's guidelines, and that was and is our intention. We walked away from our friend feeling more sorrow for him than he did for us.

We went home that night with a renewed understanding and desire to "be of good cheer." We knew we were guided to that mall that night. We knew we were in that department store at that exact moment so we could not only recognize our situation and how very blessed we were, but we were there also to lift a friend. He needed our love and support at the time far more than we needed his, and we were able to give it to him. We also learned when you focus on the needs of others, rather than wallowing in your own self pity, you boost yourself up in a greater capacity than you could by any other means. We talked all night of the beauty of this experience and what we learned. We were surrounded and filled with the spirit, and we went home different people than we had been. We talked for days and weeks about it, continuing to use the experience to remind us of our many blessings, and now, I share it with you for the same purpose.

*May we be
found among those who
give our thanks to our Heavenly
Father. If ingratitude be numbered
among the serious sins, then
gratitude takes its place
among the noblest of virtues.*

— THOMAS S. MONSON —

One Foot in the Grave

bout two years after Brant's death, there was another similar tragedy in our church—another baby drowning. The family lived in
another neighborhood at the
time of the drowning, but
they were building a home
not far from ours. Their son's
circumstance was quite different in that he continued to live
and was taken off all life support except oxygen. He was

> *No matter what the experience may be,*
> *each gives us a chance for personal*
> *growth, greater wisdom, and, in*
> *many cases, service to others with*
> *more empathy and love.*
> — RONALD A. RASBAND —

still in an unconscious and critical condition, but they were allowed to
bring him home to care for him there.

They brought him to church each Sunday, and it always seemed
they ended up sitting right around us, usually in front of us. Lyle had
accepted a position as a counselor to our new bishop, so he would sit on
the stand instead of with us in the congregation. Because our family was
so large, I always sat on one of the front rows. I felt if our children knew
their father was watching them, they would be less likely to misbehave,
and I definitely had my hands full.

It was hard for me not to watch this mother with her invalid child and wonder how it would feel to be in her position and have Brant alive. She had been made aware of our own tragedy by other church members, and I felt, even though I hardly knew her, we had common ground between us. I tried to be as friendly as possible, but she always seemed too busy with her baby and her other children to say much to me.

"Behold, mine arm of mercy is extended towards you, and whosoever will come, him I will receive." (3 Nephi 9:14) And whosoever accepts this invitation will be "encircled about with the matchless bounty of his love." (Alma 26:15)

Although they were building in the same neighborhood, they were far enough away that I wasn't aware of the constant trips they made in an ambulance to the hospital, or the paramedics being called for emergency help they needed. I learned of it after the death of their son.

He lived several months in this condition, never regaining consciousness, always fed through a tube, always critical. The mother never seemed to be bothered, but the father did. I can't fairly judge either of their hearts; I can only say what I witnessed week after week. I envied them, and yet I didn't.

I looked at my own family and who they were becoming—my two new babies, my husband and how he was able to give of himself and of his time to serve the Lord in a very special capacity—and I knew the road we had been given was the best for our family. I knew it in my mind, but I still struggled daily to accept the loss of Brant in my heart.

That struggle must have shown in my countenance more than I was aware of because not too long after the death of this family's son, the mother stopped me in the hall at church and asked if she could visit with me. We had been in the same ward for nearly a year at this time, and this was the first time I felt warmth between us. There'd been a sort of distance before. She then proceeded to explain to me why she had been distant and somewhat cool towards me. Her explanation wasn't long, but the

Learning to endure times of disappointment, suffering, and sorrow is part of our on-the-job training. These experiences, while often difficult to bear at the time, are precisely the kinds of experiences that stretch our understanding, build our character, and increase our compassion for others.
— Joseph B. Wirthlin —

last words she said are what I remember to this day. She said, "I have avoided being around you because I feel you walk around with one foot in the grave."

I was shocked and hurt at the time. I really didn't know what she was talking about—*one foot in the grave?* I certainly did not. I shared this with my husband and asked him what he thought. He said he agreed with her to a point. This caused me to wonder and ponder and never forget her words. I still didn't agree; sometimes we just can't see who and where we are. I knew how hard I was trying, but I did agree I was still sad. Nearly every day I was sad, and the sadness was focused on Brant.

Life went on, and several years passed. We moved back to our hometown, and we learned that she'd also moved away. We heard that she and her husband had divorced. We didn't see her again until five or more years later; she happened to be visiting in the same ward we attended. She recognized me and stopped me in the hall of the church. It was the first time we had spoken since the last time she'd stopped me at church. She asked me how we were doing, and I asked her the same. She had remarried and looked bright and happy.

Then I shared with her how much her words from our last conversation had meant to me. I think she was a little embarrassed and apologized

*In a world where sorrow
ever will be known,
where are found the needy
and the sad alone,
how much joy and comfort
you can all bestow,
if you scatter sunshine
ev'ry where you go.
Slightest actions
often meet the sorest needs,
for the world wants daily
little kindly deeds.
Oh, what care and sorrow
you may help remove,
with your songs and courage,
sympathy and love.
When the days are gloomy,
sing some happy song;
meet the world's repining
with a courage strong.
Go with faith undaunted
thru the ills of life,
scatter smiles and sunshine
o'er its toil and strife.
Scatter sunshine
all along your way.
Cheer and bless and brighten
ev'ry passing day.*

— Lanta Wilson Smith

for them, but I told her not to be sorry—they had become a powerful statement in my life. I explained that after a few years I had realized she was right—I did have "one foot in the grave." Once I realized this, I made some changes—great changes. Through the experiences I had, *I decided* who I would be, and did not allow circumstance to dictate who I was.

Once I got to that point, I made a decision. That decision was to *keep* "one foot in the grave," and I did it on purpose. I told her I realized that it kept me going the direction I wanted to go.

I no longer mourned for Brant in the way I had before, but I always thought of him, not with sadness, but with joy. He was my son and always would be, and I looked forward to being with him again. He was a reminder to me of the purpose of life.

"And so you see," I said, "I'm glad to have 'one foot in the grave.' It turned out to be a compliment to me."

I thought she would be flattered and happy, but she didn't seem to know what to say or how to react. I had gleaned from her words something that was exactly opposite of what she had intended for me to glean. I've never seen her again, but I hope her words became as powerful and important to her as they are to me. I hope she also has "one foot in the grave."

> *Not even
> death can take from
> us the eternal blessings
> promised by a loving
> Heavenly Father.*
>
> — Joseph B. Wirthlin —

"Are You Still Reading Those Death Books?"

Several chapters ago, I shared the experience of finding "the little white book" that taught me so much about faith. It was my time now, having read that book, to begin to grow and learn more of faith and the other laws and elements that pertain to faith. If one book could cause this much awareness in me, along with much prayer, I wondered what other books of similar nature could do.

Prayer becomes more meaningful as we counsel with the Lord in all of our doings, as we express heartfelt gratitude, and as we pray for others with real intent and a sincere heart.

— David A. Bednar —

I decided to go to a local religious bookstore. I didn't know what I was looking for, as with the little white book, but I knew I would feel it when it popped out at me. I slowly looked up and down the rows of books as I walked from one end to the other. There it was—another book stood out just as it had happened before. I took it off the shelf and knew by the way I felt that this was the book. The name of the book was *Drawing on the Power of Heaven* by Grant Von Harrison. I looked quickly through it to further confirm my feelings, bought it, and went home.

It was warming up outside, and I started a practice of letting Jordan, Tomi Jo and Angela play on the front lawn of Lyle's parents home, where we were living, while I read and waited for our other children to come home from school. Darci told me later it was something she came to expect: to drive up in the driveway and see me sitting there reading.

I read that particular book several times. I even bought several copies in paperback for my family to read and study. It taught me such a great principle on faith, but more importantly, it was a study guide to use as I practiced having faith. The author went through important steps in gaining faith and showing how to implement it in your own life.

> *As we truly humble ourselves, we will be blessed with this gift to have faith and to hope for things which are not seen but are true. (See Alma 32:21) As we experiment upon the words given to us by the scriptures and the living prophets— even if we have only a desire to believe— and do not resist the Spirit of the Lord, our souls will be enlarged and our understanding will be enlightened.*
> — Dieter F. Uchtdorf —

My life was turning and I was happy, or I was happy because I was turning my life. I was using the principle of "be of good cheer." That is a choice we make—we choose to be happy; we choose to smile; we choose to think positively about our life; and we choose to let the trials in our lives become blessings.

When I knew it was time to move on to another level of understanding, I again went to the bookstore and followed the same procedure. I found another book entitled *Spiritual Plateaus*. Glenn L. Pace wrote about the three plateaus of life, and growing through these plateaus toward perfection.

As I finished this book, I was getting stronger in my understanding of this doctrine and felt a need to know that Brant was where I had always believed he was. I was still in need of that comfort and further knowledge. In spite of all of the experiences I'd already had with Brant, and those we had as a family, I needed to ponder it all. I needed to study the doctrine I believed. I needed to know if others knew what I knew, or in other words, had some of the same experiences.

I found a little book called *Angel Children*. It was very informative for me as it supported everything I believed with scripture, something I wasn't very proficient in at that time. That book guided me to other books that taught the doctrine of life after death. There seemed to be a great interest in the subject at that time because many books were being written and published about people who had "life after death experiences" and then lived to share them. I began to read as many as I could; I seemed drawn to them.

There was a series of books written by a member of my church who had compiled stories of many people who had experiences like this. The first one came out about the same time my interest was growing. I read it and then would anxiously wait for each new book to be released. While I waited, I would read more doctrinal books on the subject, usually written by members of my church.

> Listen to the words of Christ, your Redeemer, your Lord and your God. Behold, I came into the world not to call the righteous but sinners to repentance; the whole need no physician, but they that are sick; wherefore, little children are whole, for they are not capable of committing sin; wherefore the curse of Adam is taken from them in me, that it hath no power over them. Behold I say unto you that this thing shall ye teach: repentance and baptism unto those who are accountable and capable of committing sin; yea, teach parents that they must repent and be baptized, and humble themselves as their little children, and they shall all be saved with their little children.
> — MORONI 8:8,10 —

It was during this time we moved from Lyle's parent's home and bought a five bedroom condominium. The neighborhood was nice, and the people of the ward in our church were very receptive toward us and our children. Lyle was almost immediately made a counselor to the bishop. I was also called to a position over the children in the ward as Primary President.

My husband and I attended a monthly correlation meeting with the leadership of the ward to talk about upcoming activities for the month. I would come with my manuals for my position and whatever book I was reading at the time. I carried the newest book I was reading with me almost everywhere I went just in case I had one or two extra minutes to read.

One day as I passed our bishop in the hall of the church, he stopped to talk to me about something that had to do with my calling and the children of our ward. He glanced down and noticed the book I held in my arms. He looked back at me and said in an almost reprimanding tone, "Are you still reading those death books?" I chuckled and made some lame excuse, but it really hit me hard. I was about halfway through this particular book and was finding it harder and harder to read. I had read nearly every scripture or quote many, many times with all the books I'd already read. I still loved them all, but I knew I no longer needed to read them over and over again.

I realized, through his words, that I was done. I was done with this segment of my life, and it was time to go on. I didn't need to read "those death books" any longer. I needed to read books of life and its purpose. I needed to read a book that would give me all of my answers. I decided the best books for that were the scriptures. I started reading them with as much love and passion as I had been reading my "death books." I discovered I could find my answers and the reason for life in them.

I'm still far from having all the answers, so I continue to read the scriptures every day. I have found more peace in them than I could have imagined—my purpose for life books.

It is impossible for a man to be saved in ignorance, the principle of knowledge is the principle of salvation . . .; and everyone that does not obtain knowledge sufficient to be saved will be condemned.

— Joseph Smith Jr. —

Mom's Doing Good Now,
She Only Cries Once a Day!

When our eldest son, Courtney, was nineteen, he was called to serve a two year mission for our church. We always taught him it would be a special experience to have, and he'd planned to serve a mission from the time he was old enough to understand what that meant. He'd told me, as far back as the age of four, he knew he wanted to go on a mission for our church.

> *But I have commanded you to bring up your children in light and truth.*
> — DOCTRINE & COVENANTS 93:40

The way a mission works is male missionaries can leave when they are nineteen or older; the mission is completely financed by the missionary or his family; they leave knowing they will not see their family or friends in any way for the two years they are gone; and the only contact with family is through letters and two phone calls a year on Mother's Day and Christmas.

Courtney left on his mission in January of 1996, ten years after Brant died. That was more than enough time for us, as a family and individually, to be healed. I felt that I had especially come a long way and was not in any way holding in feelings of pain. I looked forward to Courtney going on a mission. I knew what a great growing experience it would be for him and what an example he would be to his younger brothers and sisters. (Darci was happily married and had her first child.)

It was a cold, snowy day when we drove Courtney from our hometown to the Missionary Training Center in Provo, Utah. I think I started missing Courtney before we left, which I expected to feel. I was very close to my son. What I didn't expect to have was the extreme reaction after we left the MTC and for months after.

As we walked out of the building into the cold, gray, snowing weather, the heaviness and pain I felt was almost more than I could bear. I know Lyle felt very much the same. We both cried as we walked to our car.

Train up a child in the way he should go; and when he is old, he will not depart from it.

— PROVERBS 22:6 —

The weather seemed to be exactly what we felt. The snow wasn't a beautiful, white, soft snow; instead, it was a heavy, grayish, wet snow. The feeling of the weather was the feeling of my heart and that feeling stayed with me for months.

I cried more often than I wanted to admit. Our son, Matt, said it best in a letter he wrote to Courtney a couple of months later. He said, "Mom's doing good now. She only cries once a day!" I can imagine what my children were thinking, I'm sure they were thinking their mother had lost it.

I thought this was a normal reaction to your son leaving on a mission. I talked to other mothers, and I didn't think I was much worse than they seemed to be. However, I have since had two other sons go on missions, and my reaction, although I missed them extremely and I cried because I missed them, was not the same as with Courtney. I kept saying to my husband and my oldest daughter, "I feel the way I felt when Brant died." I felt that same feeling of it being final.

After Courtney had been gone for about six months, I did start to feel better. I was fanatical about writing letters, for both me and our children.

I would make everyone sit down every Sunday and write a letter. I took the letters we wrote him, then made copies of them and put them in a book along with the letters we received from Courtney. I mellowed a little by the end of the two years, but I was still more fanatical than a normal person would be.

After Courtney came home, and five months later married the girlfriend who had waited for him, I analyzed my feelings. I realized I'd had an over-the-top reaction to Courtney being gone. I believe it was because of the pain I remembered—the same feeling I had at Brant's death. It created the same feeling of loss, and I felt the same pain. Consequently, I amplified the feeling of loss and loneliness.

I knew Courtney would be returning home. I knew this was the best thing Courtney could be doing with his life, to grow and become a better individual,

Called to serve him,
Heav'nly King of glory,
chosen e'er to
witness for his name.
Far and wide
we tell the Father's story,
far and wide
His love proclaim.

Called to know the
richness of His blessing—
sons and daughters,
children of a King.
Glad of heart,
His holy name confessing,
praises unto Him we bring.

Onward, ever onward,
as we glory in His name;
onward, ever onward,
as we glory in His name;
forward, pressing forward,
as a triumph song we sing.
God our strength will be;
press forward ever,
called to serve our King.

— UNKNOWN

but I allowed my old pain to take control. I forgot, for a time, what I had learned and the decisions I had made, and I let emotion take control. I opened a door and allowed Satan to use his tools against me—something that is easy for us to allow to happen if we are not aware. We can never let our guard down for a minute. We must always be the ones in control of our life and our emotions.

Sometimes the speed bumps on life's road seem too big to get over, and they get in our way. We must remember this is but a short time in our eternal existence, and we need to keep it all in perspective. I wish I'd had that wisdom in the past. It is a hard thing to always remember, and the only way to remember is with daily reminders. I would find myself lost daily without prayer, scripture study, and looking for reasons to be happy.

Let thy bowels also be full of charity towards all men, and to the household of faith, and let virtue garnish thy thoughts unceasingly; then shall thy confidence wax strong in the presence of God; and the doctrine of the Priesthood shall distil upon thy soul as the dews from heaven.
— DOCTRINE & COVENANTS 121:45 —

I have found, through the years that you can always find someone worse off than you. Every time I start to have a "pity party," it seems I run into, or hear about, someone whose trials are so much greater than mine. I feel embarrassed that I'm not more grateful for what I have.

Don't let Satan sneak in through the back door as he did in my case with Courtney's mission. Though I was so happy for Courtney's mission, and we were greatly blessed as a family for it, I let my emotions control my opportunity for complete joy. And so I repeat, don't let Satan sneak in the back door and steal from you that which is so precious in life—the joy of the moment, the joy of the day.

And because of
your personal history,
(who you were in the pre-existent
life) you were entrusted to come to the
earth in these last days to do again what
you did before—to once again choose good
over evil, exercise exceedingly great faith,
and perform good works—and to do so in
behalf of the kingdom of God on the
earth and your fellowman!

— JAMES J. HAMULA —

In Our Hearts We Knew . . . It Was Brant

*D*arci was expecting her fourth baby and went in for a routine ultrasound. Her obstetrician discovered the thing all parents pray will never happen—their son would be born with a heart defect. This wasn't just a simple defect; in fact, he had one of the worst defects imaginable. He had a hypoplastic left heart. Hypoplastic means part of his heart wasn't there. In his case, he was missing the entire left side of his heart. They explained he would need open heart surgery within seven days of birth or he would die, if he survived birth at all. He would need a series of three surgeries over a period of about three to four years. All of these surgeries were extremely critical, and he could die in any one of them. He would be considered a critical care child most of the time.

> It is often in the trial of adversity that we learn those most critical lessons that form our character and shape our destiny.
> — DIETER F. UCHTDORF —

In spite of this news, our daughter and her husband lifted their chins and went on as normal as possible.

Joseph was born on January 29, 2005 at the University of Utah Medical Center in Salt Lake City, Utah. He was immediately transferred to Primary Children's Hospital where the surgery would be performed.

He spent the next several weeks in isolation in the intensive care unit there. It was an exciting and intense day when Darci and Brad were at last able to bring their baby boy home.

Burdens provide opportunities to practice virtues that contribute to eventual perfection.

— L. WHITNEY CLAYTON —

The care of this very sick little boy was difficult and not many people could do what these valiant young parents did. They are so special, as are Joseph's older siblings.

Joseph was born and lived through those first, very intense, critical days. At four-days-old, they planned for his surgery. Although it was nearly cancelled because the surgeon wasn't sure he would survive it, they were able to proceed and Joseph lived through it. The reconstruction they did to his heart is so complex I can't begin to explain it, nor would the normal reader begin to understand. Darci, however, has become somewhat of an expert on the functions of Joseph's heart.

In May, Joseph went into a tachycardia. His heart was beating at about 350 beats per minute when the ambulance arrived at the hospital. We live in southern Utah, and the hospital isn't equipped, nor do they have the knowledge to care for a baby like Joseph, so they prepared to life flight him to Primary Children's in Salt Lake three hundred miles away. He was in this state for several hours. As Darci and I were alone in the room with him for a few moments, his heart couldn't take it any longer, and he had a cardiac arrest. We actually could see as his spirit lifted from his body. Somehow his wonderful pediatrician managed to revive him. Joseph was gone for about ten to fifteen minutes. The important thing to know here is, to put it in the words of the life flight nurse when she learned about Joseph's cardiac arrest, "You just don't get these 'blue babies' back from a cardiac arrest." But we did, and they were able to get him to Primary Children's where he spent the next several weeks, most of it in a coma.

After a couple of weeks in the hospital, things were looking quite bleak for Joseph. Darci and Brad decided they wanted to give him a name and a blessing, which they had not been able to do since his birth because of his condition. This is something done formally at church, to give a newborn their name, along with a special blessing. This would now need to be done at the hospital.

Darci made arrangements with the hospital to allow their families into the isolation intensive care unit all at one time. Normally only two were allowed in at once, but because the hospital staff believed Joseph would probably die, they agreed to let us all come in for this special ordinance. We had to come in late at night when the hospital was quiet, and they had us enter through the back part of the unit where Joseph's room was. All of Darci's siblings gladly traveled up from southern Utah to be there. This is just what we do in our family. Brad's family was there as well, and many of them also traveled from southern Utah.

Quietly, we all filed into Joseph's room. There was a beautiful reverence about everyone that I will never forget. Darci and Brad's fathers and brothers surrounded Joseph's bed. They placed one hand on the shoulder of the person they stood next to and the other hand on Joseph. It was a sacred and special sight to see all of these men as they surrounded the bed of this sweet, tiny three-month-old baby. Darci and I stood near the door at the end of the bed, just behind my son Matthew, who stood in the circle.

> The light of belief is within you, waiting to be awakened and intensified by the Spirit of God.
> — ROBERT D. HALES —

After the blessing ended, Matt came to Darci and asked her why she placed her hand on his other shoulder during the blessing. She assured him she had not put her hand on his shoulder as that obviously would have been inappropriate to do. He insisted he had seen her hand on his shoulder. He said he was so shocked at feeling it there that he turned and looked to make sure of what he was feeling. I interrupted at this point because I had been standing next to Darci. I assured him that, indeed, Darci did not at any time have her hand on him. We all stood very solemn in that reverent atmosphere wondering the same thing— *could it have been Brant?* We can only know something like this in our hearts, but as far as the three of us were concerned, we did know that it had been Brant. I believe he was allowed to be part of this very special, sacred ordinance.

Incidentally, Joseph did live. He had the second surgery a couple of weeks later and has since had a third surgery. At the time of the writing of this book, he celebrated his fifth birthday.

By careful practice,
through the application
of correct principles, and by
being sensitive to the feelings
that come, you will gain
spiritual guidance.

— Richard G. Scott —

Special Cruise

*J*n September of 2007, Lyle and I had the opportunity to go on a cruise that was organized by the Bob Proctor seminars. Bob Proctor is a very powerful and successful motivational speaker. We first became acquainted with Bob while Lyle was working in the insurance industry. The company he worked with hired Bob to present his seminar to the company's associates throughout the United States.

For as he thinketh in his heart, so is he.
— PROVERBS 22:7 —

We met Bob while we lived in California and I was expecting our second child, Courtney. Lyle was so impressed with Bob's presentation and ideas that he wanted his parents and me to attend the next seminar that he was giving. Bob was taking the seminar to Las Vegas, so we traveled there and met Lyle's parents, who traveled from southern Utah, to attend it. It was a wonderful experience which we always remembered along with Bob's teachings. Lyle often studied and used, as well as taught, these concepts throughout our marriage. He recently became reacquainted with "The Bob Proctor Seminars" and attended another week-long seminar in Florida with our youngest son, Jordan.

It was soon after their trip to Florida that we had the opportunity to go on this special cruise. It was quite a bit more costly because it wasn't just a cruise—it was a positive-thinking cruise. Bob had invited some of the most renowned names in that business to be part of a speaking forum throughout the week we would be sailing.

Whatever, friend, you can conceive and believe, you can achieve! Success comes to those who become success conscious. Failure comes to those who indifferently allow themselves to become failure conscious.

— NAPOLEON HILL —

I have a different attitude than most on the subject of listening to so many speakers. My feelings are if you only have a cup with you, don't try to put a quart of water in it. It will only end up spilling out, and you may not retain what is most desirable to you. Therefore, I didn't attend every speaker's presentation as most did, taking copious notes, rehearsing what was taught at breakfast, lunch and dinner. I chose who I wanted to listen to and at what time. In between, when everyone else was still trying to capture every morsel they could, I would ponder in our cabin the things that were most powerful and needful to me at that time in my life. I thoroughly enjoyed this cruise— every part of it.

It was during my pondering moments that I felt inspired to write this book—something I have felt I was supposed to do from the time of Brant's death. I have told my husband often over the past twenty years, "I feel I'm supposed to write a book about my experience with Brant's death." However, either the pain was still too great, or I had not experienced all I needed to experience to write it. It was during this cruise that I came to the conclusion it was time. I never have considered myself in any way, shape, or form, a writer. However, I felt pushed, as if this was something I needed to do. Whether for me or for others, it really didn't matter; I only knew it was important for me to write my story.

As we returned home and time went on, it started to form in my mind what needed to be said. I was deeply touched and moved upon by the spirit of this cruise.

The attitude of everyone we met was, very simply put, remarkable. All of the invited speakers were equally wonderful. The foundation of what was taught was the importance of who we are and reaching our full potential. Most of what was taught coincides with my own personal and spiritual beliefs—that we are of infinite worth and that most of us don't tap into a particle of the potential of who we are, where we came from, and where we are going.

> Somebody said that it couldn't be done,
> but he with a chuckle replied that,
> "Maybe it couldn't," but he would be one
> who wouldn't say so till he'd tried.
> So he buckled right in with the trace of a grin
> on his face. If he worried he hid it.
> He started to sing and he tackled the thing
> that couldn't be done, and he did it.
> Somebody scoffed: "Oh, you'll never do that;
> at least no one has ever done it";
> but he took off his coat and he took off his hat,
> and the first thing we knew he'd begun it.
> With the lift of his chin and a bit of a grin,
> without any doubting or quiddit,
> he started to sing and he tackled the thing
> that couldn't be done, and he did it.
> There are thousands to tell you it cannot be done,
> there are thousands to prophesy failure;
> there are thousands to point out to you,
> one by one, the dangers that wait to assail you.
> But just buckle right in with a bit of a grin,
> just take off your coat and go to it;
> just start to sing as you tackle the thing.
> That "cannot be done,"and you'll do it!
>
> — Edgar Guest

One of the most interesting things about the cruise was I never, not once, saw anyone in the casinos and rarely saw anyone just sitting in the

The voice of the Spirit is described as being neither 'loud' nor 'harsh'. It is 'not a voice of thunder, neither . . . (a) voice of a great tumultuous noise.' But rather, 'a still voice of perfect mildness, as if it had been a whisper,' and it can 'pierce even to the very soul' and 'cause (the heart) to burn; occasionally it will press just firmly enough for us to pay heed. But most of the time, if we do not heed the gentle feeling, the Spirit will withdraw and wait until we come seeking and listening and say in our manner and expression, like Samuel of ancient times, 'speak (Lord), for thy servant heareth'. (Boyd K. Packer) To receive the witness of the "still small voice" sometimes can have a stronger impact on our testimonies that the visit of an angel.
— CARLOS A. GODOY —

bar. When there were breaks, the pools were surrounded with families and/or groups of people visiting, spending quality time together. I took the time to walk the ship just to note what the majority of the people were doing. I was very impressed with them. They were special, as special as the cruise. I would go again in a heartbeat.

Conclusion

$\mathcal{I}$ have heard Bob Proctor say many times, "We are not a physical body having a spiritual experience; we are a spiritual body having a physical experience." I love that; I think it is one of the most profound statements ever said.

If we can learn we are on this earth to have a physical experience and gain control over our physical body, then we can also understand we have always existed in the spirit. Our Heavenly Father

> *Thus saith the Lord God: I will give unto the children of men line upon line, precept upon precept, here a little and there a little; and blessed are those who hearken unto my precepts, and lend an ear unto my counsel, for they shall learn wisdom; for unto him that receiveth I will give more.*
> *— 2 NEPHI 28:30 —*

loved us and wanted us to have this physical experience. He knew the way would sometimes be hard for us and He knew we would learn "line upon line, precept on precept." He knew we would sometimes stumble and fall, but He is there cheering us on, telling us to pick ourselves up and try again.

He was aware some of our errors might be very serious, but He gave us a plan to be redeemed through our Savior, His only begotten son—the only perfect person to ever live who atoned for our sins.

He gave us a plan, a plan that would allow us to return to his presence. What a glorious plan.

We do have a purpose in life and I would like to suggest it is this— to prepare ourselves to meet God. When I was given the understanding to let Brant die, a very difficult, yet profound experience to have, I knew the love of my Heavenly Father and I knew I was not alone.

Although spiritual truths may appear less tangible, to the humble heart their impact is undeniable. It is important to understand that natural laws were not determined on the basis of popularity. They were established and rest on the rock of reality. There are also moral verities that did not originate with man, they are central to a divine plan which, when discovered and applied, brings great happiness and hope on our mortal journey.

— KENNETH JOHNSON —

Unfortunately, the concept sounds simple, but the way is not always so simple. Often when we take a journey, especially a long journey, we need a map. Can you imagine taking a trip across a country where you'd never been without a map to guide you? You would probably end up hopelessly lost at some point.

This is the way it is with our lives. If we try to do it alone, without guidance to get us through the rough terrain we might encounter, we will very possibly end up lost. The maps we have been given are the scriptures, coupled with prayer, and then belief, faith, hope and charity. We are taught in the scriptures that there are many gifts. The gifts I have mentioned—belief, faith, hope and charity—will be needed for our journey to ensure our safe return to our Heavenly Father.

These are the gifts that strengthened me through the trials I faced with Brant's death. When we seek diligently for all good gifts, we will always find ourselves on the right road.

BELIEF

The gift of belief is a very important step to faith. First you must believe on something and then faith is having confidence in that which you believe; it's the knowing within your heart without seeing. But you

Jesus said unto him, thou canst believe, all things are possible to him that believeth. And (he) said with tears, Lord, I believe; help thou mine unbelief.
— MARK 9:23-24 —

must *want to believe.* You must plant that seed and then nurture it. If you plant the seed, then search diligently, praying always to know the truth and believing in that truth, if your desire is righteous, then that seed will begin to grow within you. Your heart will begin to swell. This is the work you will do to begin to have faith, for we know faith without works is dead.

As you continue in your efforts of belief, you will begin to see a manifestation of the truth. You will begin to receive a witness through many ways from the Spirit. I personally call this "gifts of the Spirit." Some may refer to this as "The Law of Attraction." If your desires are good and you keep your thoughts of the thing you desire positive, if you hold a positive image of yourself and surround yourself with positive people, then you go forward, expecting to receive what you have asked to know or receive. This is belief, and to believe is the first step to faith.

I would like to share a story I read in a book just recently. The story takes place in Atlantic City and was originally printed in *The New York Herald* in May, sometime before 1921.

"She was an old woman, and when she was arraigned before Judge Clarence Goldenberg in the police court today she was so weak and tired she could hardly stand. The judge asked the court attendant what she was charged with. "Stealing a bottle of milk, your Honor," repeated the officer. "She took it from the doorstep of a downtown cottage before daybreak this morning."

> *If you think you are beaten,*
> *you are,*
> *if you think you dare not,*
> *you don't.*
> *If you like to win,*
> *but you think you can't,*
> *it is almost certain you won't.*
> *If you think you'll lose,*
> *you're lost,*
> *for out of the world we find,*
> *success begins with*
> *a fellow's will—*
> *it's all in the state of mind.*
> *If you think you are outclassed,*
> *you are,*
> *you've got to think high to rise,*
> *you've got to be sure of yourself*
> *before you can ever win a prize.*
> *Life's battles don't always go*
> *to the stronger or faster man,*
> *but soon or late the man*
> *who wins is the man*
> *who thinks he can!*
>
> — UNKNOWN

"Why did you do that?" Judge Goldenberg asked her.

"I was hungry," the old woman said. "I didn't have a cent in the world and no way to get anything to eat except to steal it. I didn't think anybody would mind if I took a bottle of milk."

"What's your name?" asked the judge.

"Weinberg," said the old woman, "Elizabeth Weinberg." Judge Goldenberg asked her a few questions about herself, then he said:

"Well, you're not very wealthy now, but you're no longer poor. I've been searching for you for months. I've got $500 belonging to you from the estate of a relative. I am the executor of the estate." Judge Goldenberg paid the woman's fine out of his own pocket, and then escorted her into his office where he turned her legacy over to her and sent a policeman out to find her a lodging place."

I learned later that this little woman had desired and mentally pictured $500 while all the time ignorant of how it could possibly come to her. But she kept her vision and strengthened it with her faith.

I wanted to share this story because, although simple, it teaches a profound message. The power we have within our minds and the strength we have through our spirit is stronger than most of us comprehend.

FAITH

It is my feeling that faith is imperative to a successful life. Faith is achieved as you work hard on the other principles. Faith is not to have a "perfect" knowledge of things. Therefore, if you have faith, you will hope for things, which are not seen, which are true (Alma 32:21, 26-43). I believe some people are born with this gift. However, if it isn't always nourished by the other principles, it can be lost.

It has been said fear and faith cannot exist in an individual at the same time. If you fear, it takes the place of faith. If you have faith, you will not fear. This was taught best in *The New Testament* when the Savior was walking on the water to meet his disciples who had started across the Sea of Galilee. When Peter saw Him, he asked the Savior if he could

Positive and negative emotions cannot occupy the mind at the same time. One or the other must dominate!
— NAPOLEON HILL —

come to him. The Savior said, "Come." Peter had nearly reached Jesus when he realized the waves were crashing around him. He immediately feared and started to sink. Peter cried out to Jesus to save him. The Lord reached forth his hand, lifted Peter up, and must have felt some disappointment when He said, "Oh thou of little faith, wherefore didst thou doubt?" (Matthew 14:22-33).

Of all the principles taught in the scriptures and throughout the ages, faith is taught more and focused on more than any other. Why would that be? Is it because it is perhaps one of the greatest principles to understand, and maybe even one of the most difficult to gain? Even the disciples of Jesus often found themselves lacking in faith. Consider the story of the Savior as he calmed the stormy seas. He was sleeping with his head upon a pillow in the rear of the boat. The storm was raging wildly, and the boat began to fill with water. Finally, in desperation—and you can imagine

Master, the tempest is raging!
The billows are tossing high!
The sky is o'er shadowed with blackness.
No shelter or help is nigh.

Carest thou not that we perish?
How canst thou lie asleep
when each moment so madly is threat'ning
a grave in the angry deep?

Master, with anguish of spirit
I bow in my grief today.
The depths of my sad heart are troubled.
Oh, waken and save, I pray!

Torrents of sin and of anguish
sweep o'er my sinking soul,
and I perish! I perish!
Dear Master. Oh, hasten and take control!

Master, the terror is over.
The elements sweetly rest.
Earth's sun in the calm lake is mirrored,
and heaven's with-in my breast.

Linger, O blessed Redeemer!
Leave me alone no more,
and with joy I shall make the blest harbor
and rest on the blissful shore.

The winds and the waves
shall obey thy will: peace, be still.
Whether the wrath of the storm tossed sea
or demons or men or whatever it be,

no waters can swallow the ship where lies
the master of ocean and earth and skies.
They all shall sweetly obey thy will:
peace, peace, be still. (169)

— Mary Ann Baker

their fear—his disciples went to him and awoke him crying, "Master, carest thou not that we perish?"

Jesus replied to them, "Why are ye fearful, O ye of little faith?" He then arose and rebuked the winds and the sea; and there was a great calm (Matthew 8:23-27, Mark 4:36-41).

Two great principles are taught here. The first is, and I repeat, "Fear and faith cannot exist in a person at the same time." The second, and perhaps the greatest principle of faith, is faith is an actual power. When faith is fully understood . . . it is an actual power. Faith has been understood periodically throughout time by man, but was always understood and used by the Savior. If faith is to be used as a power, it must be directed to the right source. In other words, it must be a faith in something that holds that power. I believe the source of that power is Jesus the Christ and I believe we must have faith in him. If we look to Christ in all things, if we believe in his words, if we truly believe Christ, our faith can become undaunted, unwavering, and unshakeable in all things. We must look to Christ and live (Alma 37:47). If we can gain this understanding, we will be prepared, and we will not fear.

It is often, after the trial of our faith, that mighty miracles can be wrought. Miracles do not create faith in us, but faith can create a miracle. That miracle, again, can only be achieved by our works as James said in James 2:26, "For as the body without the spirit is dead, so faith without works is dead also."

HOPE

For me, hope and belief go hand in hand. What would be the point of believing in something if you don't also have hope in it? Hope is a principle that is important to the very existence of our well being. When we lose hope, Satan steps in and uses his tools against us. I like to call Satan's tools the "D" words—words such as despair, despondency, depression, darkness, discouragement, disillusion, doubt, etc. However, that's not the focus. The focus is the brightness of hope, which is completely on the opposite side of the spectrum as darkness and despair. Hope creates joy, love,

Faith in Jesus Christ and a testimony of Him and His universal atonement is not just a doctrine with great theological value. Such faith is a universal gift, glorious for all cultural regions of this earth, irrespective of race, color, language, nationality, or socioeconomic circumstance. The powers of reason may be used to try to understand this gift, but those who feel its effects most deeply are those who are willing to accept its blessings, which come from a pure and clean life of following the path of true repentance and living the commandments of God.
— DIETER F. UCHTDORF —

selflessness, courage, happiness, caring for yourself, as well as others, etc. It is my personal belief that it would be virtually impossible to have faith without hope; for hope is the beginning power of faith.

CHARITY

Charity is the last and probably the most important gift to be found with as we come to the end of our sojourn on earth. As a matter of fact, if seeking happiness is our journey, then charity would surely be considered our destination. What is charity and why is it so important? This would be best answered in the words of Mormon as he spoke to the people he loved and eventually died trying to guide: "If a man be meek and lowly in heart, and confesses by the power of the Holy Ghost that Jesus is the Christ, he must needs have charity; for if he have not charity he is nothing; wherefore he must needs have charity. And charity suffereth long, and is kind, and envieth not, and is not puffed up, seeketh not her own, is not easily provoked, thinketh no evil, and rejoiceth not in iniquity but rejoiceth in the truth, beareth all things, believeth all things, hopeth all things endureth all things. Wherefore, my beloved brethren, if ye have not charity, ye are nothing, for charity never faileth. Wherefore, cleave unto charity, which is the greatest of all, for all things must fail—but charity is the pure love of Christ, and it endureth forever; and whoso is found possessed of

> *Therefore, I would that ye should be steadfast and immovable, always abounding in good works, that Christ, the Lord God omnipotent, may seal you His, that you may be brought to heaven, that ye may have everlasting salvation and eternal life, through the wisdom, and power, and justice, and mercy of Him who created all things, in heaven and in earth, who is God above all.*
>
> — MOSIAH 5:15 —

it at the last day, it shall be well with him." (Moroni 7:44-45) He goes on to admonish us to pray with all the energy of our heart to receive and be filled with "this love." By "this love," he means the "pure love of Christ," which is the meaning of charity. If you think of all the words Mormon has used to describe what charity is, and you were to say in one phrase what they meant all rolled into one, they would surely mean "the pure love of Christ."

I have become the person I am today because of the experiences I've had in my life and the choices I've made, (some better that others). We are all in that same boat. We are who we are because of experiences, choices, and attitudes. Henry B. Eyring said, "You make choices every day and almost every hour that keep you walking in the light or moving away towards darkness. We need to become consciously aware, in our daily lives, of the thoughts we allow ourselves to have, because these thoughts will ultimately become our actions, which in turn dictate who we are, where we are going, and who we will become."

Over the past three years and during the time I have been writing this book, I have had the opportunity to serve as the Young Women's President in the ward of our church. The girls in this organization range in age from twelve to eighteen. It has not only been a great privilege, but I have also felt the importance of being a constant example to these beautiful young women.

> *Professor Harold Hill from "The Music Man" said, " You pile up enough tomorrows, and you'll find you've collected a lot of empty yesterdays." There is no tomorrow to remember if we don't do something today. Let us relish life as we live it, find joy in the journey, and share our love with friends and family.*
> — THOMAS S. MONSON —

The Young Women's organization in our church has a theme which we repeat each week as we meet together. We say this in unison at the beginning of our meetings. I find myself repeating it in my mind,l quite often, throughout the week. I love the theme. I love what it stands for, and I love the words. I love saying it.

I would like to take the liberty of changing one word and then share it with you. I hope it will be something that you might like to continually repeat as a reminder of who you are, as well. The word daughter is being changed to children.

We also have a motto in our Young Women's organization. It is "Stand for Truth and Righteousness." We ask one girl to stand and lead us in the theme. As *she* stands up, *she* says, "Please stand for truth and righteousness." At this, we all stand and repeat the theme, which is:

We are children of our Heavenly Father
who loves us, and we love Him.
We will stand as witnesses of God
at all times and in all things, and in all places
as we strive to live [our] values, which are:

FAITH, DIVINE NATURE, INDIVIDUAL WORTH, KNOWLEDGE,
CHOICE AND ACCOUNTABILITY, GOOD WORKS, INTEGRITY *and* VIRTUE

We believe as we come to accept and act upon these values,
we will be prepared to strengthen home and family, make and
keep sacred covenants, receive the ordinances of the temple,
and enjoy the blessings of exaltation.

Many times since Brant's death I've been asked how I survived the loss of my child. I have heard more than once, "*I just couldn't do that.*" It took a little time but I finally realized that, although Heavenly Father gave me the opportunity to release Brant at the time of his death, the decision for Brant to die was not mine to make. When Brant came to me while his life was being maintained by machines . . . that was his message. Brant was *"willing to stay . . . but it wasn't up to us; it was up to our Heavenly Father."*

The thought I have shared with those who can't imagine going through such an ordeal is *I didn't have a choice in whether my son lived or died, but I did have a choice in how I handled it.*

After my experience with my youngest daughter, Tomi, and the life-changing events that happened at that time, I especially became aware of this. I made a conscious effort to make the choice mine and *"be of good cheer"* as we are taught throughout the scriptures.

BRANT AND (FATHER) LYLE WOOD   PAINTING BY LORI WOOD

About the Author

*L*ORI ANN WOOD was born in Las Vegas, Nevada. Her family moved to St. George, Utah while she was in elementary school. After graduating from high school, she met and married her husband, Lyle. They have eight children who have been the joy of their lives. They currently have twenty grandchildren with the hope of more still to come.

Lori focuses her life around her family first, her church second and then developing her talents. She has taken art classes for several years at Dixie State College in St. George where she and Lyle now reside. A few of the portraits she has done have been shared in this book. Most of the portraits she has done have been of her children and grandchildren, as these are her favorite subjects. She hopes to continue with her art as well as the development of other talents.

Visit Lori at www.AMightyChange.com or www.LoriAnnWood.com.

The portrait of Lori is by Del Parson.

Bibliography

Adams, Sarah F. 1805-1848 (Hymn book; "Church of Jesus Christ of Latter Day Saints", pg. 100) Pg. 40

Andersen, Neil L. (*Ensign*, Nov. 2008, pg. 13) Pg. 123

Ashton, Marvin J. 1915-1994 (*Ensign*, May 1992, pg. 18) Pg. 69

Baker, Mary Ann (Hymn book; "Church of Jesus Christ of Latter Day Saints" pg. 105) Pg. 208

Beck, Julie B. (*Ensign*, May 2010, pg.10) Pg. 120

Bednar David A. (*Ensign*, Nov. 2008, pg. 44) Pg. 183 (*Ensign*, Sep. 2007, pg. 60) Pg. 168

Benson, Ezra Taft 1899-1994, Pg. 28, 41, 83, 162

Bibesco, Elizabeth Asquith 1897-1945, Pg. 101

Bliss, Philip Paul 1838-1876 (Hymn book; "Church of Jesus Christ of Latter Day Saints", pg.131) Pg. 78

Brooks, Phillips 1835-1893, Pg. 15

Camus, Albert 1913-1960, Pg. 111

Clayton, L. Whitney (*Ensign*, Nov. 2009, pg. 12) Pg. 196

Clayton, William 1814-1879 (Hymn book; "Church of Jesus Christ of Latter Day Saints" pg.30) Pg. 98

Corbridge, Lawrence E. (*Ensign*, Nov. 2008, pg. 36) Pg. 93

Harold B. Lee 1899-1973, Pg. 1, 134

Lund, Gerald N. (*Ensign,* May 2008, pg. 32-34) Pg. 169, 170, 171

Martino, James B. (*Ensign,* May 2010, pg. 101) Pg. 19

McCloud, Susan Evans (Hymn book; "Church of Jesus Christ of Latter Day Saints," pg. 220) Pg. 54,

McKay, David O. 1873-1970, Pg. 132

McMullin, Keith B. (*Ensign,* Nov. 2008, pg. 75) Pg. 104, 119

Monson, Thomas S. (*Ensign,* Nov. 2008, pg. 61, 67, 76, 85, 86, 87) Pg. 68, 86, 102, 110, 116, 137, 143, 151, 161, 176, 211

Nelson, Russell M. (*Ensign,* Nov. 2008, pg. 92) Pg. 131

Nicholson, James 1828-1876 (Hymn book; "Church of Jesus Christ of Latter Day Saints," pg. 89) Pg. 139

Oatman Jr., Johnson (Hymn book; "Church of Jesus Christ of Latter Day Saints," pg.241) Pg. 175

Phelps, William W. 1792-1872 (Hymn book; "Church of Jesus Christ of Latter Day Saints," pg. 2) Pg. 126

Rasband, Ronald A. (*Ensign,* May 2008, pg. 11) Pg. 167, 177

Roosevelt, Eleanor 1884-1962, Pg. 2

Scott, Richard G. (*Ensign,* Nov. 2009, pg. 6) Pg. 198

Shakespeare, William 1564-1616, Pg. 75

Smith Jr., Joseph 1805-1844, Pg. 112, 187

Smith, Lanta Wilson (Hymn book; "Church of Jesus Christ of Latter Day Saints," pg. 230) Pg.180

Snow, Eliza R. 1804-1887 (Hymn book; "Church of Jesus Christ of Latter Day Saints," pg.273) Pg. 58

Thayne, Emma Lou 1924 (Hymn book; "Church of Jesus Christ of Latter Day Saints," pg.129) Pg. 4

Uchtdorf, Dieter F. (*Ensign,* Nov. 2008, pg. 21, 23, 24) Pg. 48, 49, 62, 71 (*Ensign,* Nov. 2009, pg. 4, 24, 55) Pg. 60, 184, 195, 209

Unknown (Hymn book; "Church of Jesus Christ of Latter Day Saints," pg. 249) Pg. 191

Walker, Charles L. 1832-1904 (Hymn book; "Church of Jesus Christ of Latter Day Saints," pg. 96) Pg. 24

Wattles, Wallace 1860-1911, Pg. 92

Wirthlin, Joseph B. (*Ensign* Nov. 2002 pg. 82) Pg. 51 (*Ensign,* Nov. 2008, pg. 26-28) Pg. 84, 91, 94, 97, 100, 115, 145, 173, 174, 179, 181